What 

Saying About

Uniting Church And Home

This is an important book. It offers a cooperative, integrated, and covenantal approach to life and ministry rarely seen in these fragmented, individualistic, and parochial times. Its Biblical foundations, Reformed outlook, and practical emphasis make it refreshingly substantive while at the same time startlingly relevant.

The responsibilities of the home ought to be facilitated by the church not co-opted. Likewise, the centrality of the church ought to be embraced by the home not resisted. This remarkable blueprint for symbiosis shows us how to strike that kind of essential balance.

George Grant, PhD, Dlitt
President, Bannockburn College
Franklin, TN

The time has come to apply the proven insights gained from the home schooling movement to the reformation of the local church. Eric Wallace makes a worthwhile contribution in his new book to that end. I recommend it.

Gregg Harris
Author, *The Christian Home School*
Pastor, Household of Faith Community Church
Gresham, OR

Within Christianity two dangerous extremes predominate. The first would pit the local church against the family by segregating children from their parents and allowing the youth culture of our day to drive ministry activities. The second would react to this crisis by rebelling against the authority of the local church. Eric Wallace demonstrates that God desires the family and the local church to operate in perfect harmony. His book is a refreshing look at how to achieve the biblical balance.

Douglas Phillips
Family Vision Ministry
San Antonio, TX

Eric Wallace shows that he understands both the crucial nature of the Church as the Body of Christ and the reasons why, as we enter a new millennium, that community is failing to fulfill the vision of its Lord. His understanding of households as the critical focus of local church life, together with his approach to equipping households for ministry, holds the promise of a reformation in the way we structure and grow our churches, and may just help to point the way toward real revival in our day.

T.M. Moore
President, Chesapeake Seminary
Linthicum Heights, MD

In a day of raging confusion about ministry-models, Eric Wallace speaks with clarity about the necessity of uniting church and home.

This approach expresses the covenant concept of home and

church working together to tradition the faith to the next generation. This timely book is, indeed, a blueprint for covenant community.

Susan Hunt
Director of Women in the Church
PCA Christian Education & Publications Committee
Atlanta, GA

In this age of "high tech" we need to be "high touch." This is especially true in terms of ministry. Mr. Wallace has demonstrated for us in practical terms what it means to walk by grace through faith in terms of relationships within the body of Christ. I believe this book presents a great remedy to the "business-as-usual," bureaucratic form of ministry which builds walls between people rather than tear them down. It is wonderful to read a book on ministry which carries the "sweet savor" of the gospel throughout its presentation.

Rev. Benton Taylor
Grace Presbyterian Church
St. Marys, GA

These ideas that have been expressed to me over the years in embryonic form have finally been fully developed and written in a clear and precise manner. This book clearly defines an innovative and challenging vision for the renovation of the modern church.

Rev. Floyd Hall
Penn's Woods United Methodist Church
Pittsburgh, PA

Uniting Church and Home by Eric Wallace is truly an innovative approach to the growing dilemma that is facing many of the churches in America today. The reader will be faced with viewing the "facility based-program oriented church, in a new and refreshing way. Is a church on every corner really the answer for America's needs? Or, is it a family based deprogrammed church? I tend to believe that it is the latter. Eric's insights are rich, challenging and I believe a timely message to those of us who are pastoring today. It is time for a revolution to take place in the church, a revolution that must first come in the home. A revolution that will restore fathers to their place as the pastor over their families. When this begins to happen, I believe that revival will sweep the church in America. This book is must reading for anyone concerned with where the church is going today."

Dr. Bob Roach
President, Freedom Seminary
Pastor, Calvary Worship Center
Author, *The Father's Heart*
Port St. Lucie, FL

Martin Luther, Calvin, Zwingli, and other reformers restored the purity of the church. Today a new reformation has begun to re-establish the institution of the family along Biblical lines. Eric Wallace's book is a major player in the reformation of the family by defining the spiritual role of the fathers and the household in the advancement of the kingdom of God.

In his book, he gives a pointed analysis of the problem and practical solutions of how the two major institutions of the family and the church should biblically work together to advance the Kingdom of God.

Eric Wallace is a reformer in the sense of reestablishing the culture that properly esteems the role of the family in spiritual advancement of the kingdom of God and particularly the role of the father in restoring America.

This book is a breath of fresh, clear, Biblical air in the pervasive and pre-

dominant staleness of the age-segregated, family-divided church program approach to success.

Pastor Stephen Ong
Author, *Scripture Activities for Family Enrichment*
Age-Integrated Sunday School Curriculum
Greeley, CO

"...Impressive and clear...Plymouth Rock Foundation and its Christian Committees of Correspondence are dedicated to urging the institutional churches to minister to the needs of the people in their local neighborhoods and communities, and to train men of God to become political leaders as in the days of the First American Revolution.

Your book is a welcome and refreshing contribution to that end...Your focus on the heart is of particular significance."

Neil F. Markva
Plymouth Rock Foundation
Springfield, VA

Eric has been a great encouragement and help to me as we have worked to build Godly households in and through this local body. The material presented here is helpful and practical. I am especially challenged through the many stories and examples about what others are doing.

Stewart Jordan
Pastor, Redeemer Presbyterian Church in America
Madison, AL

ERIC WALLACE

Uniting Church and Home

A Blueprint for Rebuilding Church Community

Uniting Church and Home

Published by Solutions For Integrating Church and Home
P.O. Box 630
Lorton, VA 22199
571-642-0071

Produced by Hazard Communications, Inc.
P.O. Box 568
Round Hill, VA 21042
540-338-7032

ISBN 0-9667311-0-7

Printed in the United States of America

To My Beautiful Wife, Leslee

L.L.P

Contents

Acknowledgements

To my Heavenly Father, I give praise and glory for giving me the time, ability, and strength to write this book.

I acknowledge Leslee, my wife, whom God has used to help me grow in my understanding and appreciation of heart-level relationships in everyday life.

I want to thank my parents, Lightsey and Louise Wallace for all their help, especially for teaching me the value of hard work, without which I could not have finished this book.

Les and Carol Stadig have been sources of encouragement and help for which I am grateful. Their heart-level training of their daughter, now my wife, has proven irreplaceable in moving this vision forward.

Ron Bossom, my pastor, close friend, and counselor has helped me find balance and gave me freedom to test the waters.

I owe gratitude to Ben Taylor, one of my best friends, who has helped me to understand and cultivate grace in life and has contributed greatly to the development of this vision.

Mike Welborn has been a constant source of support through the years, pushing me along when I was ready to give up.

Luke Godshall has been an encouragement through our many afternoons discussing aspects of the vision, especially working with fathers.

David Hazard has been my faithful coach, helping me get the vision in print. I would also like to thank Helen Motter for her help with the multi-faceted headache of editing. David and Helen made the book a reality.

The Harvester elders (Ron Boenau, Ron Bossom, Mark Hayes, Larry Pratt, Bruce Stanly, and Lightsey Wallace), have provided an atmosphere wherein I could freely develop my vision and ministry.

The HTS volunteers, including, Dave and Nicky Dickmann, Eddie and Lynn Estalote, and Dan and Carol Matz, have helped or supported me in many direct and indirect ways.

Many others have contributed through practical encouragement, counsel, proofreading, and countless other ways: Dan Bartel, Dan Dorianni, Tom Eldredge, Michael Farris, George Grant, Floyd Hall, Gregg Harris, Susan Hunt, Stewart Jordan, Neil Markva, Steven Ong, Doug Phillips, Kerry Ptacek, Bob Roach, Dennis Rupert, John Thompson, John and Catherine Velleco, Tom Wenger, and John White.

Foreword

The Evangelical Church, parachurch and educational community faces at least three great challenges. How can we have a pedagogy that more accurately reflects Biblical norms? How can we communicate a Christian message free of legalism? How can our programs and structures be delivered from the endemic individualism of our culture?

Eric Wallace provides a corrective vision of a Biblical holism for church, home and education. This is a book filled with a Biblical theological argument for the household concept which will result in a re-thinking of our paradigms for doing church and education. But it is also filled with more than theory, it is loaded with practical steps for implementation and many illustrations of how his proposals work out in the life of church and family.

This book is a must read for Evangelical parents, church leaders, and educators.

Dr. John H. White
President, Geneva College
Former President, National Association of Evangelicals

Introduction

Many commentators predict difficult times are ahead for our country and the world. I believe, however that the church's best days are yet to come.

As I look out across the landscape of churches in our country I see a reformation taking place. This book describes the vision and outworking of this reformation. The information in this book will be a great help for Pastors, leaders and church members who are enthusiastic about becoming more conformed to the image of Christ. Restoring the biblical model of the household and doing ministry that equips the family to impact the world for Christ has a most enticing aroma.

The reader should be prepared to accept how the church's neglect of families has effectively crippled ministry. However, the reader will be graciously encouraged by what is happening in a growing number of churches that have stepped out from behind the shadows of their own "traditions" into the light of personal heart-level relationships.

Entirely new approach? No. But perhaps it is new to this age when church life has become focused on canned formulae for success like growth by numbers rather than equipping for spiritual maturity.

This is not a book about an abstract theory. Numerous real life examples and practical suggestions effectively qualify the work as a "how to" guide. Appendix C directly addresses problems associated with change and recommendations for overcoming them.

Special treatment is given for integrating into church ministry the strengths of the fastest growing resource of "together" households in the nation, home school families.

In many ways, I am still learning about these principles and their application myself. I do not have all the answers, nor do I claim to have them. I pray that through this book virtually every reader might be energized and encouraged to try at least one suggestion or to develop their own new ideas to expand and strengthen household ministry in their church … and get ready for reformation.

PREFACE

When I was hired by Harvester Church to design a home-school assistance ministry in May of 1989, I did not know that God would use it as a catalyst to develop a vision to help revive the way many churches go about ministry, but that is exactly what He has done.

Though the home schooling movement played an initial role in leading me to my present work — uniting the church and the home — my present ministry, and this book, is not aimed exclusively at helping home schoolers. Far from it. Every pastor and parent can understand and apply these truths. I would summarize these truths in the following simple statements: We are called to integrate the spiritual values taught at church into our lives at home; and we are called to integrate the love and support of the family into the life of the local church. The church and family need each other!

As I developed the ministry at Harvester, for instance, it became apparent that the needs of home-schoolers were not just academic. Although Harvester Teaching Services (HTS) had done much to help with academics, I discovered that our families really wanted and needed help with basic every-day life issues: relationships in the household, discipline, authority, leadership, roles, priorities, serving one another, being able to apply biblical principles, and so on. We provided a resource center, classes, and activities that equipped parents, but the reality was that we were still not able to get to the core of the issue, which was the heart! Some of the churches I visited for ideas on how to help home-schoolers had already discovered and met the challenge that I was just beginning to understand. It became apparent that the church as a whole was failing to disciple through relationships.

Quick-fix programs are seen as the solution to today's problems in society and in the church. I could see that the church had bought into a numbers-equals-success mentality that devalued the slower process of discipling through relationships.

As a result, my own understanding of how the church should minister began to undergo a transformation. Were my programs really helping people? Were parachurch ministries and government agencies really supposed to takeover the vital role of the local church to fulfill people's basic needs?

Then a simultaneous discovery took place. First, on my part as HTS director, and then on the part of many Harvester households, we saw that the needs of the home-schoolers were not unique to them! All households needed help in these areas, and many who did not home-school were benefiting from "home-school ministry."

Most parents we worked with were not raised in Christian homes and had little understanding of how their faith applied to everyday life. The effects of home-schooling are so far-reaching in household relationships that parents need more than a book, class, or video tape to understand it. The concepts of applied Christianity are so foreign to most parents that they need to see it lived out to understand it enough to apply it in the home. Indeed, many parents have little or no ability to evaluate problems and come to biblical conclusions! The average church is incapable of meeting this need. If this is the state of the average evangelical household—and I believe it is—how does this bode for the future of the church? How will the children in these homes surpass their present level of maturity to establish more godly generations?

I was not alone in asking these questions.

As I pondered all of this, I began to witness in the home-school community an outpouring of interest to see home-schooling support brought under the umbrella of local churches.

While I was developing HTS and studying these matters, other home-school leaders and churches found out what Harvester was doing. At the time, very few churches hired a staff member solely to orchestrate a home-schooling ministry. Even though I think we were weak in the area of discipleship, Harvester's commitment stood out—and still does. This gained Harvester international acclaim.

In 1992 I met Mary Pride (one of the pioneers of the modern home-school movement) in Colorado. We talked for three hours about Harvester. This meeting produced an offer on my part to write feature articles about Harvester and church supported home-schooling for her magazine, Practical Homeschooling, with its worldwide circulation of 50,000. I did this for one and a half years.

The Practical Homeschooling articles were the opening of a BIG door into the catacombs where people retreated because they were turned away by the church due to various levels of disagreement on home-schooling, or more frequently over conflicts in ministry. These households called me to learn how they could best appeal to their leadership to develop a commitment to home-schooling or a household ministry approach.

On two occasions I flew out to California to work with churches there. Even one parachurch ministry in Orlando, Florida, contacted HTS for assistance. (After years of trying the traditional youth-group approach, they realized that the way to reach inner-city youth was to work through churches that discipled parents to home-school their teens.) Recently, Leslee and I traveled to Minnesota to visit one church whose resource center was inspired and started with some help from HTS.

Over time I read volumes of material on home-schooling and household-based ministry. As I met more pastors and home-school leaders, a shift became apparent in the equipping people needed. It used to be that most of my calls were from individual home-school parents—mostly mothers—interested in how to appeal for home-schooling support. But over the past four to five years, the preponderance of calls have been from pastors who are looking for more than advice on home-schooling. They see that home-schooling is raising key issues at the core of a household approach to ministry, and they need help transforming their church.

It has been a personal vision of mine that God would use me to bring His people together in all their diversity to work on the root problems that affect the church and our nation. This vision is being fulfilled in the work that I am doing with churches, bringing them together on these timely issues. Through my contacts, and with Pastor Bossom's help, I was able to put together three conferences that showcased for pastors what was happening in these areas: "Reviving the Church Through Home- Education Ministry," "Transforming the Church Through Household-Based Ministry," and "Uniting Father, Family, and Church Through Family-Based Ministry." Because of the relative newness of these matters, much material was presented that surpassed where Harvester was. We were learning too! We were able to give a little, but I think we were able to learn a lot! Our primary contributions to these conferences came in the following forms.

First, God showed me a maxim to help people appeal to their church leaders to support them in home-schooling or developing a household approach to ministry. The maxim is that "**Some parents home-school, but all parents home-educate.**" According to Deuteronomy 6, this is true.

Second, from Deuteronomy 6 I developed a paradigm for understanding what it means to be a "home-educator": God's plan is accomplished over generations through heart-level relationships that are nurtured in everyday life. For too long, parents have only thought of their teaching responsibility as being something that they do today. They fail to see the effect they are having on future generations. When parents, whether they home-school or not, understand the breadth of this vision, they see even more clearly that in order to accomplish this goal they need teaching, discipleship, accountability, and the host of other needs that only the church is ordained to meet.

Further, this paradigm is more than a plan for parents working with their children; it is a household discipleship vision for the entire church: singles, single parent families, blended families, orphans, widows, the divorced, teens—everybody! Thus, another bridge was built to help pastors see how a home-education ministry could help develop unity among the body of Christ and, most importantly, advance a household approach to ministry!

The calls and requests for "support for home-schooling" were really calls for the church to do a better job discipling its people, but especially in equipping fathers to lead their households.

This maxim and paradigm have been useful in developing home-education and household ministry with individuals and churches in forty-four states.

What I see happening in churches of all denominations is a movement away from the hurried, superficial, age-segregated, activity-laden ministry. They are moving toward a whole different approach that centers on freeing up the body to build godly households through heart-level relationships and age-integrated ministry. As leaders begin to consider the implications that are brought forth through the household discipleship vision, they are led to some challenging conclusions about ministry. The equipping that people need cannot be provided through the traditional age-segregated approach. Indeed, many parents find the traditional model at odds with what they try to do in the home during the week.

History teaches that all major revivals ironically have not come from the institutional church. And so, though this is not a book only for home schoolers, I would be remiss if I did not acknowledge on behalf of the church the debt of gratitude we owe to this movement. Is has helped bring fresh insights into how we can integrate spiritual values in the home. By humbling parents so that they have the attitude to learn, strengthening the leadership of the father, and by showing the value of household units as tools for ministry, the church can be strengthened. Strong households are the core of strong churches, and strong churches are the foundation for outreach to our communities, nation, and the world.

Churches in ever-increasing numbers are seeking to move away from methods of ministry that are in reality working against the establishment of faithful generations. A renewed focus on multi-generational vision, heart-level relationships, and nurturing in everyday life (the household discipleship vision) are the slogans of this revival. Thus, we see the movement away from the traditional age-segregated approach toward an age-integrated household approach. The obvious unity among brothers and sisters of different denominations is just one of the many definite signs that this approach is of the Holy Spirit.

I hear about more pastors who are waking up to this revival in the church. These are men who are reading, praying, and fasting about these matters. God is blessing their ministries not so much in numerical growth—for there is surely some of that—but in a far better way: He is building a level of maturity in the church that has not been seen in recent memory.

I believe that this revival in the church has the potential of dwarfing all others in history because what is happening extends beyond mere revival to reformation of church life. Revival can occur without reformation and it usually dies with the current generation. But as the church reforms the way it teaches, lives, and ministers we have greater hope to see many generations build on our successes and grow in faithfulness. Many reading this book will probably agree with me that what our churches need is not simply revival but full-fledged REFORMATION.

It is such a blessing for me to be a part of what God is doing through the vision presented in this book. The household discipleship vision is producing reformation, and to quote a famous theologian, "We ain't seen nothing' yet"!

Will you join me in moving this reformation forward? The fields are white unto harvest. Go therefore and reap!

Eric Wallace
January 1999

The State Of The Church Today

Part One

In many churches across the country numbers and financial giving are up. These factors appear to indicate that all is well. Appearances, however, can be deceiving. Although our ministries are running smoothly, more and more pastors and families are experiencing a sense of disconnection between the life of the church, its purposes, and especially between church and home. Chapter one takes you into the minds and hearts of a pastor and his flock to expose the primary problem which is a failure to integrate spiritual values into life and home.

A House of Living Stones

chapter I

It is a gloriously bright, sunny day as Randy Hines, Senior Pastor of Trinity Community Church, arrives at his office on Monday morning. After a brief conversation with his secretary, Judy, he carefully pours a cup of coffee and carries it into his office. Warmly ensconced in his high-back desk chair, he notices that there are already three phone messages vying for his attention.

The first message is from the Stewarts. Ward and June Stewart joined Trinity only seven weeks ago. Ward is a new believer who made a profession of faith when visited by one of Trinity's evangelistic teams. June, a Christian since childhood, struggles with her husband's spiritual immaturity. They find themselves in Pastor Randy's office once or twice a month seeking help after major arguments. Ward has been trying to convince Randy that Trinity needs another Sunday school class that will help husbands and wives deal with marital conflict. This message has reminded Randy that Ward expects him to call with an answer on Monday morning.

The second message is from Ethel Higgins. Ethel came from a traditional church background. All of her forty-two years were spent in the Episcopalian church because of her love for the brilliant choral and instrumental music. Ethel, however, has been attending Trinity since coming to their Christmas cantata nine months ago. Randy notices Judy's handwritten memo: "Concerned about new direction of music." At the request of a growing group of younger members, Randy has allowed some experimentation lately with more contemporary styles of music in the worship service. Apparently, Ethel does not like it. With a stressful exhale, Randy moves that message to the bottom of the pile.

The third message is from Jeff McClintock, one of the elders. Randy knows that Jeff and his wife, Sandy, are having difficulty with their fourteen-year-old daughter, Sarah. Just three weeks ago, Sarah was arrested at school with cigarettes and alcohol. Sarah's defiant heart has devastated Jeff and his wife. It was only a year ago that Sarah won the award for memorizing the most Bible verses in her Sunday school class; now she seems to be in constant trouble, throwing the entire family into turmoil. Randy went over one night and counseled the family from 9:30 P.M. until 3:30 A.M. Randy sighs as he looks again at the memo, which reads "URGENT." That can only mean further difficulty.

As Randy ponders the problems represented by these messages, his thoughts wander to the relationships within his own family. Over the years his wife, Michelle, has developed a bit of resentment toward his ministry. The demands of going out to church-related meetings four to five nights a week, evangelistic visitations, mediating crises—often into the wee hours of the morning—has left little time for Michelle and the children. "How strong is my marriage?" he wonders. Concerned about his meager salary, Michelle constantly raises the question whether or not she should go out and get a job, but she fears what the more conservative members of the church might think.

His wife is not the only person on his mind, though. He thinks about his three children, Elizabeth, Joe, and Kara, who are now twelve, fifteen, and nineteen respectively. Admittedly, he spends hardly any time with them anymore. Kara, his oldest daughter, now in college, is dating a non-Christian. His son, Joe, is more involved in sports than ever. Sports is to Joe what ministry is to Randy, his love. Joe is spending more and more time on the soccer and football field and less and less time at home and especially, at church. Recently, a rift developed in their relationship when Randy told Joe he could not play soccer on Sundays but had to attend church services. Randy's youngest daughter, Elizabeth, is spending more time with her friends but seems to show a genuine desire to grow spiritually. Joe and Kara are much more complacent about spiritual matters.

Randy lays his messages aside and picks up the church's attendance and giving reports for the previous day. Sipping on his now lukewarm coffee, he notices that Sunday school attendance was up to 170. "Wow, that's an increase of twenty people," he says out loud. Attendance at the morning worship service was up from 250 to 300. The new singles ministry was also well attended. To add to his delight, the report shows that giving was up. The church needs $6,000 a week to make budget, and this week's offering was $10,000! This is good news since the previous week's offering was rather low, and they have been working hard to put money into their building-expansion program.

But these apparent signs of success cannot lift Pastor Randy's soul from the turmoil of doubt that something just is not right. He begins to wonder how effective Trinity's ministries really are. The messages on his desk represent problems similar to those he has faced with other church members. Most troubling is the fact that these problems seem to occur over and over, sometimes in the same family. Randy knows there will always be problems, but he is concerned over an apparent lack of spiritual depth. People in the church are not learning from their failures. They seem complacent and stagnant; they show little desire to get involved in ministry.

Of further concern is the fact that Trinity has no program for single parents, yet single-parent families were listed on a demographic study as the second-largest outreach group in his area. His staff is already maxed out. Can he really burden them to develop yet another ministry?

Seminary never prepared Randy for this onslaught of fears, doubts, and frustrations. The barrage of questions he asks himself causes his soul to squirm in a spat of confusion. There appear to be rather large conflicts between the church's ministry goals and the results in members' lives. Is he doing ministry "right"? Offering activity after activity seems to make only a marginal difference in the lives of his people and leaves him physically, emotionally, and spiritually drained.

Scene Two

Randy Hines is not the only one asking questions this Monday morning. Sitting at his breakfast table, Walter Murphy butters his toast in silence while pondering his wife's question: "Should we talk with Pastor Randy about our concerns?" Walter and his wife, Mary, are looking at the direction their family is going and are seeing many conflicts with the direction of their church. They feel the church is actually working against what they are trying to accomplish in their home.

Walter was one of the charter members of the Trinity men's ministry, organized after he and five other men returned from a Promise Keepers rally. He feels the ministry has only been helpful to a point, and does not challenge or enable him to strengthen the strained relationships in his home and family. Mary, meanwhile, enjoys the fellowship provided through the women's Bible study but often struggles to see how the lessons being taught bring her into deeper fellowship with God.

Both Walter and Mary think they are doing a decent job raising their children but deep down question the closeness of their children's relationship with God, which often seems lukewarm. As parents they believe they are doing all of the right things—dropping their children off at sports activities, youth group and Sunday school. But they are still concerned that their children simply do not thirst spiritually. As parents they seem to have lost touch with their children, who spend most of their time away from home at school, with friends, and even at separate church activities. Walter and Mary have trusted the church over the years to teach their children how to grow spiritually. Now they are wondering if the church really has a relevant impact on the lives of their sons and daughters.

Walter and Mary agree that Pastor Randy and the other leaders teach interesting classes and preach good sermons, but they often fail to make the connection between what is taught and how it works out in real life. They know that Trinity is billed as a "family-oriented church," yet the various programs seem to have little to do with preserving and strengthening the family. Rather, it seems to the Murphys that the church is doing more to prevent family unity than to promote it as everyone heads off to their separate classes and worship services. Sunday mornings have simply become another busy morning in the family's hectic schedule.

As they continue to eat their breakfast, Mary reminds Walter of the times years ago when each of their five children would bring home Sunday school work sheets every week. They had realized then it was virtually impossible for each of their young children to internalize all of that material week after week. It was simply too much to digest and implement into everyday life. They had often wondered over the years what their children were really learning at Sunday school, and if it was making any difference in their lives.

They further question how they can help others outside of the church's programs and activities. They want to be more involved in bringing the gospel to the unchurched in their community, but they are kept so busy going to various church activities, they do not understand how to accomplish this. Instead of being "out in the world" sharing the gospel, they feel locked in to church activities that keep them focused on their own church. Ironically, everything that happens at Trinity Community Church seems to happen at the church building itself, not out in the greater community.

This particular Monday morning, Walter and Mary have come to a crossroads concerning their church and the effectiveness of its ministry. They are asking each other some tough questions: "What really is the church's role? Does the church serve us, or do we serve the church? How is the church supposed to equip us as believers? What place do we as parents have in the equipping process? How is all of this division of our family into separate programs in line with Trinity's identity as a family-oriented church?"

Pastor Randy Hines is about to receive another call this morning from a couple in the church with some serious issues to discuss.

Churches Aren't Walking the Talk

If you were in Pastor Randy's shoes, what would you say to Walter and Mary Murphy? Do any of the Murphys' questions have a familiar ring? Whether you are a pastor, parent, or individual, chances are you have asked yourself the same questions at one time or another. Why are there so many conflicts in the church today? Why does the church seem so out of touch with the daily lives of its members?

What is particularly tragic is that the world around the church is thinking these same thoughts. The lack of connectedness in the local church with the lives of its members is marring the reputation of our Lord and His gospel. The world wants truth that is integrated with life and have stopped looking for it in the church.

In spite of today's sophisticated world, people are still shattered by the ravages of sin. They are looking for a place where they can be forgiven and accepted—a place where they can belong. People who are aware of their failures want to be open with others, free to share their deepest concerns. They are looking for purpose and fulfillment—not simply more activities to fill up their already bulging schedules. Many who have tried to find that fulfillment in the church have been sorely disappointed—betrayed by the empty promises of well-intentioned but misguided churches. The life-changing message of the gospel is reduced to hypocrisy in the eyes of the world because they see that Christians do not always walk the talk. These Christians keep themselves busy within their churches but fail to convincingly live out their faith among the unchurched. In our increasingly liberal culture, Christians are often viewed as narrow-minded, judgmental, and intolerant—clearly in need of transformation themselves.

What is a Church to Do?

Pastor Randy and the Murphys are typical of many pastors and church members today. They see the problem, but they do not know what to do about it. As Christians, many of us are also wondering what God's purpose is for the church today. We have supported expensive programs, more beautiful and elaborate church buildings, and increasingly professional presentations for worship services. Yet many of us feel disconnected with others in the church, even with our own children, as every person tries to find their niche within a distinct and separate program designed just for them. We lead very divided lives already, with so many parents working long hours away from home, and children away at school, in extracurricular activities, or just hanging out with friends. Even at church, our children usually go off to their own Sunday school classes and youth group meetings, and we as parents have little contact with what they are learning there. We ask ourselves, "Must the church be at the mercy of our modern culture that tends to divide families into separate activities all the time? How will our children learn true Christian values if most of the time they are being influenced by their peers and by the increasingly non-Christian values of the present culture?"

I propose that there are alternatives to continuing to "do church" as we have come to know it. In order to clearly understand these alternatives, we will be looking at how the early church fathers understood and taught about the church as a community of faith. In 1 Peter 2:5, the apostle Peter wrote to the persecuted brethren of Asia, saying that they were as "living stones...being built up a spiritual house."People in that day were very familiar with the massive temples where worship was centered. The Greeks had their impressive columned temples to worship their pantheon of gods. The Jews, of course, were familiar with the splendor of the Temple in Jerusalem, the priesthood that cared for it and interceded between God and the people. Peter wanted the Corinthians to understand that God does not live in temples built by human hands—He lives in us, His people.

What Peter was saying to these first-century Christians is just as true for us today. God does not live in our church buildings. WE are the CHURCH. WE are the NEW TEMPLE! Gone are the inanimate walls and curtains. Christians are the walls and curtains. The foundation is not a huge bolder but Jesus Christ Himself. As believers we receive our life through Jesus Christ, the only foundation stone. We thus become living stones: a holy priesthood. We serve God with our unique spiritual gifts, and as we serve, we build God's spiritual house.

Notice how Peter connects the imagery of building and stones to the House of God. We are not all different, constructing our own building in our own way. We are anchored and unified in Christ. We find our ultimate identity in Him. Instead of doing our own thing, going our own way in ministry, we are to work together, helping each other, complementing each other in ministry, so that the lives we build look like a beautiful, well-planned structure and not a slapped-together junkyard shack.

Ironically, the church today is right back where it was at the time of the apostles. We struggle to understand the church apart from a physical building, and yet our lives as Christians are ineffective because we restrict our ministry to narrowly individualized programs that leave little room for integration of family and church life. Instead of a beautiful temple, our building is a hodgepodge of individual stones "doing their own thing," where parts often do not connect.

What Would an "Integrated" Church Look Like?

Now that we have begun to consider the problem, you might be asking, "What are the alternatives, then?" Can modern churches truly accomplish the goal of creating "a house of living stones" as Peter described it? Just what is an "integrated" church in today's world?

Before I tackle the previous question, I need to define a term I believe is essential to understanding the concept of an integrated church. That word is "household." As I have worked with others in helping churches to become integrated, we have found it important to use the term "household," rather than "family," when discussing the organizational units of successfully integrated churches. The word "household," as I define it, means much more than simply "family." A household may consist of a nuclear family—Dad, Mom, and kids—but it also refers to single-parent families, couples without children, and men and women of all ages who are unmarried or widowed, some of whom may choose to join to another household. In other words, it is any group of people in the church who live and fellowship together.

Each separate household then becomes a vital part of the larger household of the church. An integrated church first seeks to incorporate every church member into an individual household where they can relate more intimately to other Christians than is possible in a large church setting. Then each person can more successfully become an integral part of the broader church family or household.

The following is a real-life account from a young single in my church, who only began to understand his Christian faith when he became integrated into a household. As a part of a household within the church, he was ministered to in a way that he had not previously experienced by simply going to church by himself. I will share many more stories later from various Christians who have been blessed by a glimpse of what it means to be a part of a "house of living stones." The individuals and churches involved describe a kaleidoscope of images. Their experiences are not identical, for the Holy Spirit works creatively in each situation to help every church discover how to best meet the needs of its members, and to meet the needs of the community in which the church resides.

Why I Lived With the Boenaus

by Mark Hayes

I grew up in a Christian home and accepted Christ as my Savior at the age of seven. Growing up in the church, I went to Sunday school, vacation Bible school, sang in the choir, etc. I knew the Bible with my head but had a shallow relationship with the God of the Bible in my heart. To put it simply, I was self-centered.

I finished high school, went to college, and got married five days after college graduation. The marriage revolved around me and my career. We went to church every Sunday and after a few years I became a deacon. But things were going sour. Though I professed to be a Christian, I did not really know how to live the Christian life in a way that pleased God. I was more interested in what pleased me. I knew my marriage was not doing great, but I was not concerned—at least not enough to change my ways. Well, the bottom fell out after seven years. My wife filed for divorce and I was crushed. God broke my pride and I repented. But despite true repentance and a real change of heart, my attempts at reconciliation failed and we were divorced. My wife married someone else after a couple of years.

God continued to work in my heart. I started attending the Harvester in January 1989. I wanted desperately to be married but knew I needed to learn godly ways. God especially used the Biblical Principles for Living class to teach me how to apply His Word to my life. I learned so much, but there was still something missing. I had not paid attention to my parents' marriage. I did not know how a Christian marriage should work. I wanted to see a Christian household "in action."In the fall of 1990, I asked the elders if any of them would consider allowing me to live with them for a while in order to learn from them about how a Christian household works. One of the elders agreed.

So in November of 1990 I moved into "room 4"of Ron and Barb Boenau's home (Andy and Susie had rooms 2 and 3). I became a part of the household, eating meals with them, sharing in their household devotions, raking the leaves and playing in the snow. I saw how Ron and Barb spoke with each other, dealt with their children, dealt with their households and with their neighbors. I remember how Ron would wake everyone in the house on Sunday mornings with lively Christian music; it really helped start the day. But I also got to see the household "warts and all."In one particular instance one of the children had deliberately disobeyed a standing rule of the house. I saw Barb show her grief at the sin, and how Ron, using scripture, gently but firmly confronted the sin and led the child to repentance.

God used the Boenau household to show me more of my weakness. On more than one occasion I had to ask forgiveness for something I had done or said. In all of this, God used Ron and Barb, and their constant reference to His Word, to change my attitudes and thinking about marriage, leadership, true agape love, and what it is to be a godly man.

The Lord continued to teach me in the spring of 1992. He answered my prayer—I got married. I've now been married five years and we are richly blessed. God has given me a wonderful relationship with my wife and we have three little children. He used the Harvester and especially the Boenaus to prepare me for marriage. God taught me to serve, to lead, and to love Him before He answered my prayer. I would highly recommend to any single who desires a godly marriage, but is not sure that they understand God's principles for marriage (and life), to seek such an arrangement where they can see a godly marriage modeled before them.

Mark learned a valuable lesson about how God wants to work through other Christians to help shape us into His image. The church is the place God has designed to do this. God has chosen the church as the only place where He can fully connect with His people. It is true that He wants us to relate to Him as individuals, but He also wants us to be an integral part of His body—the church—in order to grow together, and to reach out to a hurting world with the gospel. It is through the church that we model Christ before one another and a watching world.

The church, however, is not a building: it is people! The most important work of the church will always take place through God's people, wherever they happen to be—in their homes, at work, in the marketplace. **When the church rediscovers its identity as God's "household"—a network of integrated living stones—then the world will begin to see the witness of God through the church as never before.**

This book will look at a "blueprint" for restoring the household of God. We will look more carefully in chapter two at what the New Testament means in describing the church as a "house of living stones" and how our modern churches often fall short of this ideal. We will examine what a "household", or "integrated" approach to church means, and how reorganizing a church in this way can bring untold benefit to every member, as well as the unsaved in the community. We will not only share the vision of creating integrated churches, but will also discuss the practical aspects of how one goes about accomplishing this goal: how to present the concept to church leaders, and specifically what steps to take in order to engage every member in the process and make the transformation successful.

Please be aware that I am going to emphasize the concepts of household relationships to such an extent that you may begin to think that I am opposed to ministry programs. This is not the intended message of this book. I believe programs can be useful tools in ministry when they are built upon and kept in balance with the principles presented in this book. I am in the process of learning about these exciting principles and their application. I do not have all the answers and this book certainly is not the ultimate and last word.

As you consider this life-changing matter—for yourself and your church—I would ask that you keep your heart and mind open to the leading of the Holy Spirit. Some of these ideas may be difficult for you, and you may not fully agree with all of the conclusions I have drawn as I have traveled the country sharing this vision with others. Even if this is the case, I beseech you to at least consider the picture as a whole. Study the scriptures with humility and a heart open to hearing the voice of God. And most of all, be patient—with yourself and with others who desire to see God's best for their church. We may not agree on every particular, but my hope is that we can move ever closer to God's perfect plan for the Body of Christ on earth.

Our current understanding of the church's identity is limiting full-range, effective ministry. Instead of a living, loving and integrated organism, the church has become an organization that divides its people and fosters competition among ministries. These factors do not allow for regular, meaningful interaction that unites church and home. This chapter looks at how age-segregation and division began and ends with a call to unite in purpose.

The Strongest Structure

chapter 2

"Here's the church and here's the steeple, open the doors and see all the people." Remember that little Sunday school rhyme? Knowing this rhyme and the accompanying hand motions were so ingrained in me and my classmates that it almost represented a "rite of passage." This little ditty was one of the first things I memorized in Sunday school. No one ever stopped me when I did it repeatedly—enjoying the grins and glee of any adult nearby. No doubt you have probably had the same experience.

Like me, maybe you had the noble responsibility of polishing all the Sunday shoes for your family on Saturday evening so that everyone would look nice for "church" the next day. Perhaps like you, I grew up being taught many things about the identity and work of the church that do not wash theologically. As seen in these two examples, one of the errors was in thinking that the church was a special building.

As I learned more about Christianity, I began to wrestle with some contradictions. I learned that we who are saved ARE the church, yet I still found myself and others saying that we were going TO church. Did Jesus die for a building?

I wondered why the place where we worship is called God's "house" or "the sanctuary," when the Bible teaches that our hearts are the sanctuary and home of God. Traditional hymns such as "Take Time to Be Holy" seem to indicate that there are times when we aren't holy! As far as our position before God, Jesus' atonement makes us holy 100% of the time. We need to strive to bring our actions into conformity with this truth every minute of every day.

To this day, I constantly find myself falling into those old habits of thinking formed in my earliest years about what the church is and is not. I do not think my experience is unique. From our earliest days, most of us have grown up with an unbiblical concept of what the church is.

We grew up thinking that the church is a building. God's Word says the church is His people.

We grew up thinking that church activities occur mainly on Sunday morning or Wednesday evening, forgetting that a man talking with his neighbor is a church activity, or a mother going shopping with her daughter is a church activity.

We grew up thinking that God somehow lives in these buildings, but His Word says that He lives in our hearts.

We grew up thinking that the room where God's people assemble to worship is the sanctuary, when the Bible teaches us that our hearts are His sanctuary.

These and other contradictions are so ingrained in our minds that they are hard to eradicate. Furthermore, they have brought about immense confusion in the body of Christ that has seriously impeded ministry. I would go so far as to say that this misunderstanding has presented a whole different paradigm for knowing how the church is to function.

When the identity of the church is transferred from living people to inanimate buildings, the table is set for a serious feast of hypocrisy and confusion. The church becomes a place where we go to be holy and give God His due so that we can go on with life as usual the rest of the week.

To the world this flawed understanding pigeonholes the church as a place for "perfect" people, or more realistically, a place where hypocrites go to feel good about themselves. How can the world think otherwise? They never see the "church," because its activities are largely confined to a building. Too many unsaved see Christianity as a clique that meets for self-congratulation or theological debate or purely social activity, and has little to do with the struggles of everyday life.

The irony is that the world, those who are indifferent to Christianity, have the same view of the church as we do. I think it is safe to say that in many respects, they know us better than we know ourselves.

These erroneous thoughts are the recipe for confusion. It seems God's people are confused about who they are, and most importantly what the church is. For many Christians, the apostle Peter's description of the church as a "house of living stones" has become a spiritual-sounding metaphor that is difficult to relate to the modern church as we know it.

If we want to see the church truly become the living, breathing, life-giving representation of Christ on earth, then we need to be willing to let God work through us to rebuild His house—from the ground up.

So You Want to Build a House...

If you were to build a house for your family, you would not start by hammering two-by-fours into the dirt hoping that the walls would stay anchored. The first light gust of wind would render them useless. The first thing you would want to do (or have your builder do) is lay down a solid foundation for the structure.

Then, as you started to build, you would want to keep building your house upward from that solid foundation, taking care not to extend the structure beyond its foundation. Such poor workmanship would ultimately lead to collapse. Also, you would have to keep in mind that each part of the structure would need to be connected to all the other parts. Failing to connect each piece of the structure to the others would also lead to collapse.

Did you ever play with Legos as a child? I remember how I tried to build walls by stacking one Lego block right on top of the others instead of building them so that one block would bridge two others. When I did it this way, the walls always seemed to fall over and did not provide any strength for the structure. But when I finally learned to link the pieces together in an alternating pattern, the walls would gain great strength from the foundation. These blocks were integrated! I remember how difficult it was to knock the walls over when they were built in an integrated fashion. The foundation held them together as they themselves were being held together by one another.

Furthermore, remember how the strongest walls were built with the smaller blocks and not the big, long blocks? This is significant when we start to consider the rebuilding of the living, breathing house of God. We can think of the smaller blocks as representing people, not buildings or programs. People make the strongest walls when linked together in love and common purpose and are built on the same foundation. People who share a common vision are bound together by love and sacrifice and anchored in the endless strength of our Lord Jesus Christ—the firm foundation who holds us all together.

This is exactly what the church must do to build a "house of living stones." It must build using the living materials that God has given in such a way that they interconnect one with the other.

The Disconnected Church

If our "church" experience is relegated to the formality of Sunday mornings, evenings, and Wednesday nights, we miss the real life aspect of what it means to be a community. If our members are all scattered into their little individualized cubbyhole programs, we miss the household atmosphere that God intended. And consequently, the church loses its impact upon the world. When homes and families are divided—as a matter or course—the church loses. When there is little time for church members to develop relationships around real life, the church becomes a collection of ingrown special-interest groups. How is it that a person can walk in and out of Sunday services week after week but never get noticed? When identity is based on belonging to certain groups—Bible studies, Sunday school classes, couples' clubs, youth group, and the like—this is often the result.

What has happened in many cases is programs have become the life of the church taking the place of relationships. **We must remember that if relationships were strong to begin with, many programs would be unnecessary.**

The proliferation of age-segregated programs began with Sunday school in the late 1800s and youth group in the early 1900s. The key elements that were at work in their founding are true of other programs we see today.

Sunday school

Sunday school was founded in Britain in the late 1700s by

Robert Raikes. According to Kerry Ptacek in *Family Worship*, "Raikes viewed Sunday School as a means to reach the children of poor parents who had rejected the gospel" (p. 63). The idea soon caught on in America. By the early to mid 1800s, the Methodist, Lutherans, Congregationalists, Presbyterians, and Baptists all had their own Sunday school ministries. No longer were Sunday schools just an outreach for unchurched youth; they began to serve as part of the regular teaching program of the church.

L.J. Wilson, a Southern Presbyterian, dissented from the view that Sunday School was superior to home instruction in the Bible. "...on Sabbath morning they are hurried off to Sunday school where the teacher strives for thirty to forty minutes to teach them lessons they ought to have been taught at home during the week. And this is all the religious instruction the little ones get. What will be the effect upon the coming generation? It is a sad subject to contemplate."

Wilson's fears were substantiated and his assessment of Sunday school vindicated. In the 1980's the Lilly Foundation funded a series of studies of the decline of mainline Presbyterianism. It was assumed that the decline was related to a decline in Sunday school participation, which seemed to precede membership decline. A sample of adult church members and non-church members who had grown up as Presbyterians was asked about Sunday School attendance. Unexpectedly, it was discovered that both groups were equally likely to have been regular attenders of Sunday school. From the standpoint of social science, this finding indicates that Sunday school was not particularly effective. The study probed further and found that while adult church membership was unrelated to Sunday school attendance, the experience of religious instruction in the home correlated very positively with adult church membership. (Ptacek, p. 65)

Youth Group

The youth subculture that is so prevalent today has its foundation in the early twentieth century when psychologist G. Stanley Hall coined the term "adolescence." According to Christopher Schlect in *A Critique of Modern Youth Ministry*, Hall believed that "teens ought to be separated from those older and younger than them. Moreover, like most evolutionists, Hall also taught that each generation is or should be superior to the previous one, and therefore needs to break free from those who precede it. In practical terms, this thinking has come to mean that rebellion is youth's destiny. Hall, and many social psychologists after him (even continuing to the present day), viewed this rebellion as a positive thing" (p. 5).

For the most part, the church accepted these developments, allowing the youth subculture to move into the church. Youth rallies, Bible clubs, and camps were the staple of several parachurch youth ministries. While these activities provided Christianized titillation to the youth, they produced very little in long-term fruit. How could they? The segregation principle upon which these youth meetings were built was by design to instill a break from tradition of preceding generations.

Youth group was not the only program to be born out of the union between education and age-segregation. The church has largely bought into it lock, stock, and barrel by starting additional groups that further isolate and insulate each part of the church body.

The Life of a Program

Like most things, programs have a life-cycle. The excited individual who starts the program has a genuine vision for meeting the need (not necessarily the same as administering a program). Before long, however, the original leader burns out or moves on to other things and leaves the program in the hands of one who may not have the same vision or gifts. Like the Energizer Bunny, the program keeps on going, even when there is little or no need for it.

As churches grow, these individual programs become more numerous. Tragically, the identity of the church becomes a smorgasbord of programs instead of a household of interdependent people or a body as Paul describes us in I Corinthians 12.

Further, the member's vision of the church is colored more by what he can get instead of what he can give. The choice of which church to join is often made based upon how many programs a family or individual likes. When the programs that make those people happy are gone or even "tweaked", they often go shopping for another church. There is very little commitment to relationships in God's household. Life-giving relationships therefore suffer.

In the end, success is often defined as having good attendance, and exciting and fun activities, but not necessarily changed lives.

Howard Snyder tells us in his book, *Liberating the Church,* that "If the church is seen primarily as an institution, its ministry will be largely institutional and program-oriented. But if the church is viewed as a community, its ministry will be person-oriented, focusing on building structures of human interaction. And in this perspective, the structures of family, church and neighborhood are most basic. All are fairly intimate forms of human community based on face-to-face relationships. Together they provide the glue of society" (p. 129).

A look at a typical Sunday at most churches should spark concern as to how vital, nurturing relationships are being honored. Further, how is the church equipping or even encouraging leaders to take greater steps toward maturity?

On any given Sunday morning, an average household of

four will receive the following teachings: one adult Sunday school class, two children's classes, and the sermon. That is four different teachings, and we have not reached Sunday or Wednesday night yet! On Sunday or Wednesday night, add at least one class for each parent. Then the children will go into two classes.

On a conservative estimate, that is six, at the most ten teachings (depending on household size) that a household is responsible to implement in their lives! Given how busy the average household is during the week, especially the hectic work schedules of most fathers and many mothers as well, how can parents be accountable to work through all of this teaching in one week's time? The church is shoveling out information at an incredible rate. What about the all-important modeling, or example that is required to cement the application of truth? The personal discipleship that is necessary to model a truth is also necessary to evaluate the heart response.

When various households and individual members within the church do not connect, the following problems occur. First, the church becomes like a gas station. Everybody stops in, "fills up," and speeds off. This leads to eclecticism, where the church becomes a collection of individuals and programs with little unified core vision. Its identity is wrapped up in a hodgepodge of all its programs. These well-intentioned programs, designed to help specific types or categories of people, ironically become tools for ingrowth and exclusivity because they define the church as an organization to help those specific people. What happens, then, when a church doesn't have a program to meet the needs of a specific individual? That person assumes there is no place for them.

It is impossible for any one church to provide enough programs to meet the needs of everybody in a community.

Churches that try to be all things to all people this way ultimately experience burnout of the twenty percent of the people who do eighty percent of the work. Bitterness and hard feelings often follow as members fear that the church will sink like a ship if a particular program is modified or terminated. To "save the ship," others volunteer to plug the holes in the leaking vessel so that the program can go on. Eventually, however, the cycle repeats itself. Through each cycle, the sense of purpose, energy, and vision diminishes.

A second problem that arises when integration is lacking in the church is when individuals feel they are only there to be used by the church. There probably isn't one person reading this book that hasn't at one time or another experienced this one! Keeping all these programs going requires a lot of commitment. People often are led to serve in a program out of a sense of guilt, rather than clear direction from God. "Well, it's my turn now." I must confess that I myself have at times taken up a responsibility because I felt shamed into it. When this is our motivation, we might say to ourselves, "Everyone will think I'm shunning responsibility." So we become reluctant, begrudging volunteers who learn to smile when our heart is screaming to the contrary. What makes accepting responsibility so difficult for many people is that they don't see how the program is relevant for REAL LIFE.

A further hazard inherent to programs is the constant pressure for numbers. "How many people did you have?" America's fascination with the "bigger is better" mentality has unfortunately become the measure of success in many churches and ministries as well. When certain activities turn out few numbers, the volunteers automatically think that what they did was not important or not "blessed." This performance standard tragically seeps into an individual's relationship with God, and they worry that if they don't do well as a leader of a certain program, they somehow are less acceptable to God.

In both of these scenarios, we see that there are too few living stones to share the load of ministry. A few do all the work while many sit around watching it all happen.

From Competition to Oneness in Purpose

If leaders, households, and individuals within a church are integrated, then we can eliminate these problems and the destruction caused by competing agendas. Think of competing agendas like two gears meshing together that grind the living stones. Competing agendas lead to power struggles, beginning within the ruling board on down through the volunteer ranks. Which program or activity will get the most money in this year's budget? These battles have had disastrous consequences. Some people get disgusted and simply walk out. I know of one church that split over whether to spend money for curtains or a piano. These kinds of public displays turn committed believers into church hoppers. Those who stay may become judgmental, having won the confrontation. Worst of all, the name and reputation of Christ is dishonored. Our humble and serving Savior is, in effect, removed from the church. So while the doctrine and building remain, the spirit of competition rules.

In order for a church to avoid this clash of competing agendas, every member and household in the church needs to have a common vision, a common purpose. Yet a church cannot hope to achieve a common purpose if it is not integrated.

As we proceed to chapter three to a discussion of the purposes of the church, bear in mind that for a church to establish a common purpose, it must first acknowledge the ideal that every member and household be built upon the solid foundation of Jesus Christ. Only then can every member and household work toward achieving an interconnectedness with one another. During this process all the parts are strengthened and held together as the church moves forward to establish its own particular purposes and focus. **As a church begins to reorder its priorities to fall in line with Peter's picture of a "house of living stones," I believe it will begin to experience a new oneness and love and common purpose. Only then will it truly have an impact on those outside of the church as others begin to see how God's people love one another.**

The church will more perfectly reflect to the world the words of the apostle Peter: "You are a chosen people...a people belonging to God, that you may declare the praises of Him who called you out of darkness into His wonderful light. Once you were not a people, but now you are the people of God" (1 Peter 2:9-10, NIV).

Unified purpose is key to effective ministry. Fragmentation within families and the body in ministry dilutes the purposes of the church. By reviewing several key purposes of the church, we can more easily see that our approaches to ministry have actually moved us away from carrying out our purposes. This chapter will discuss five basic purposes and eight corresponding barriers presented by our current dis-integrated approach.

Becoming One In Purpose

chapter 3

Although I have never been there, the pictures I have seen and the stories I have heard about the Boeing aircraft plant in Everett, Washington, amaze me. In the late 1960s Boeing set out to build the largest passenger jet in the world. They also wanted that plane to carry its passengers the farthest of any jet and in the most comfort. The result was the well-known Boeing 747.

Anyone who has had the treat of flying on one of these leviathans, or even looked at one through the large windowpanes of an airport concourse, can appreciate the 747 as a miraculous accomplishment. As one who has flown on many 747s, including one nonstop flight from London to Hong Kong, let me say the experience is a thrill.

A 747 can carry anywhere from 350 to 500 people at a time (depending on configuration). The most recent version of the 747 has a maximum take-off weight of 875,000 pounds and can fly in excess of 600 mph nonstop from Los Angeles to Sydney in just over fourteen hours! It takes twenty-one months to assemble the 4,500,000 items required to build a 747. It's amazing that something so big can fly at all.

Boeing's purpose—to build the largest passenger aircraft in the world—not only became reality; the 747 is now the icon of the most advanced form of transportation in the world. While efforts of other aircraft companies to compete with the 747 continue, the proud lady is still the crown jewel of the traveling public.

Imagine the incredible amount of planning, cooperation, and focus that it has taken to design, build, and maintain this industry leader for almost thirty years!

It started with clear purposes. Boeing engineers wanted to build a plane that would carry large numbers of people over longer distances in greater comfort. They built upon these purposes with very clear plans that necessitated precise adherence by thousands of people. This orchestrated precision has remained the same for over thirty years.

Would such a successful program have originated from unclear purposes? Clearly defined purposes made it possible to pull together the right team of people to build the jet efficiently. Each of these people has a special role that fits into the overall plan so that the purpose can be attained. Imagine what the outcome would be if one-third of the workers thought they were assembling parts for a 747, one-third for a DC-9, and one-third for a twin-engine Cessna. The conclusion is obvious. Everybody involved in the project must understand the overall purpose and see how their role is vital to the achievement of the much bigger purpose. The person who builds one of the engines is just as important as the person who wires the cockpit or installs the lavatories. Every person is crucial and can find fulfillment in his or her unique contribution.

When we look at our churches, do we see 747s, twelve-passenger commuter planes, or something in between? Do we see something that was built upon clear purposes or something that was built piecemeal? In reality what we often see in the church are several concurrent and conflicting purposes that inevitably lead to division and disintegration of the body.

We see the leadership charge in one direction and the people wander in an opposite direction.

How can the church, with all its individual members and households, become focused together in purpose?

The Core Purposes of the Church

What is the church's purpose? Is our purpose to win everybody to Christ? Is our purpose to build a big building? Is our purpose to have enough programs to meet everyone's needs? Let us go back to the proverbial drawing board and look at some big purposes of the church, as defined by the Bible.

Purpose #1:
To glorify God (I Corinthians 10:31; Psa.73:25)

God our Father is the sovereign, all-powerful, all-knowing, always-present Creator of the universe. He is so powerful that He only needed to speak in order to bring all things into existence. All things exist at His explicit command. He knit each of us in our mothers' wombs so that we might glorify Him. It is He who provides the rain, the sun, and our next breath.

When Adam turned away from God, Jesus, God's Son, humbled Himself and came as a baby with the purpose of dying that we might have life again. Our response to so great a God can only be love and an overwhelming desire to glorify, honor, exalt, and worship Him. We owe our very existence to Him; therefore, it is our duty and privilege to glorify our Creator. Glorification, honor, and worship are more than Sunday morning activities!

These should be the hallmark of our everyday lives.

As we purge our pride and selfish desires and begin to look at every situation as one in which we can glorify the Living God, we fulfill our design and find fulfillment and joy. Furthermore, God uses the process to prove to the world that there is a Living God who cares deeply about His creatures.

Purpose #2:
To walk with God (John 10:27-29; Romans 8:11)

This essentially means relationship. God wanted Adam to walk with Him day by day. As the two walked in the garden, God revealed many things to Adam. Adam, however, yielded to the temptation to know more than God had chosen to reveal to him, and he took a shortcut that meant giving up his relationship with God.

God does not want His church to take shortcuts as Adam tried to do. The relationship between God and His church is one that only grows when the church slows down to listen to God. Because God reveals Himself to us slowly, we must slow down to listen. We cannot expect God to change us when we are chasing our own selfish desires and going on with business as usual. God is not a track coach, urging us to run faster and faster. It takes us a lifetime to get to know God. For us to mature individually and corporately, we must dedicate ourselves to the disciplines of a regular walk with God and regularly give primacy to God through prayer and meditation. As the church does this, we will once again reflect the glory of our God and King and be flashing neon signs for the power of the gospel.

Purpose #3:
To serve and support one another (Acts 2:43-47; Galatians 6:2)

By this I mean true fellowship. Love is upheld in the scriptures as the greatest virtue. Love is a sort of truth-detector in the church. In 1 John we learn that if we say that we love God but hate our brother, the love of the Father is not in us. How will those around us know that we are Christians? It is by our love for one another.

But love is not some flaky emotion. Love finds its definition in actions like commitment, sacrifice, and bearing one another's burdens. This type of love can only be demonstrated and thus defines true "fellowship". This means spending time with one another in the course of everyday life. This is hard to do when most of the life of the church is locked up within four walls on Sunday. When fellowship is secluded in this manner, relationships within God's household are shallow, disjointed, and unreal.

The fellowship of the early church that we see evidenced in the New Testament was quite pervasive and dwarfs what we typically see today. There are many verses that develop the theme of "one-anothering" and the importance of hospitality. These people ate and drank together. They visited each other's homes frequently. Today we have redefined fellowship as short surface conversations that occur between the services on Sunday morning.

In the first-century church it appears that hospitality was used as the primary method of church evangelism. It is very hard to develop deep, meaningful fellowship outside of the milieu of everyday life and the home. It is difficult to love a person whom we do not know all that well.

Purpose #4:
To bring God's message to unbelievers (Matthew 28:19)

Evangelism is far more involved than simply giving a "canned" gospel presentation. Evangelism is an essential part of the much bigger discipleship process. Discipleship must include living out God's principles so as to bring God's message to bear upon the creation and lives of unbelievers. As God's representatives on earth, we are to bring His principles to bear upon all of life. The unbeliever is looking for changed lives, and changed lives are the greatest advertisement for the gospel.

Evangelism includes living out the gospel in the company of believers and unbelievers alike. God has sovereignly and strategically placed us around people whom we can reach out to. These people are our neighbors, co-workers, bank tellers, and gas-station attendants. **When evangelism becomes a distinct program divorced from a way of life, new believers often suffer spiritual starvation because the focus and concern of the Christian becomes pinpointed to an event—a prayer to receive Christ—and not to a lifelong discipling relationship.** Unbelievers can sense this lack of connection. A good friend of mine, Ben Taylor, has a refreshing perspective on evangelism. **He reminds me that we are more like midwives than salesmen, helping to birth a new life rather than simply persuade a person of its benefits.**

I would add that our evangelistic purpose is even broader than described above. Throughout history, until recently, the church was the place where people in need—especially non-Christians—received food, clothing, medical care, and shelter. The church was society's Red Cross. Along the way the church gave up these responsibilities and retreated into its fortresses. Since that time, the church has perfected fortress life detached from the hurting people outside its walls. This retreat has shamed the name of our God who has answers to the problems of unbelievers. When we carry on church life behind these fortress walls, we give unbelievers a picture of a God who is smaller than their problems, who is impotent and unconcerned.

Purpose #5:
To disciple believers to maturity (I Peter 5:1-5; I Timothy 3:2; 5:17)

Discipleship is an all-encompassing, life-dominating activity. It is a process, not an event. The Bible uses family relationships to describe how a Christian is discipled, because the kind of intensive love, care, and training that parents give their children represent the same way to treat the new Christian. In a world that idolizes efficiency and results, we tend to grow impatient with this vital aspect of the church's purpose. We cannot shorten a process that by its very nature takes a lifetime.

As a new believer cuts his teeth on God's Word, he begins to discover his own identity as a living stone. Understanding God's will and design for how we serve Him is a process of trial and error, testing, praying, waiting, and even failing. This can be daunting, especially when done apart from a discipling relationship. Encouragement and patience from other Christians are vital for continual growth. A sermon or Sunday school class on spiritual gifts, while helpful, does not have the same impact as a one-on-one, heart-level relationship.

This process of discovery is multi-faceted in its effect upon the body of Christ. While a new believer is discipled and seeking his place in God's household, he discovers truths and has mini-awakenings, all of which are best shared within the body, because what he learns can help others to grow—even those who are more mature! God uses us as we grow. We do not have to wait for the finished product. That will only come in heaven. We are all in process, and therefore in need of discipling relationships. It's as if we all "rub off" on each other. This rubbing-off process actually strips away dirt and grime, effectually shining each living stone and moving it to its place in the living, loving body of Christ. It is this cycle of loving, learning, living, failing, and overcoming that makes up the life of the church!

Barriers to Achieving These Purposes

The view of the church as a building, as discussed in the opening of chapter two, has affected church life in many ways. Having looked at some of the core purposes of the church, let us turn our attention to some common barriers to becoming one in purpose and how they affect the church.

Barrier #1:
The church has become separated from real life.

We behave one way on Sunday morning and another way the other six days of the week. How many times have you been asked on Sunday morning how you are doing and you have replied "fine"—all the while knowing that you were not over the argument you had with your spouse the night before?

We give an appearance of having it all together, but in reality we know we are struggling with many sins. When the church is separated from real life, we open the door to hypocrisy. We become swallowed up in a fantasy world, or "evangelical ghetto" as some say, where it is understood that everybody is OK. We are either fearful or too proud to admit that we have needs, because we conclude that admitting our needs will somehow affect how we are viewed by our fellow brothers and sisters. We therefore lose perspective on what it means to have empathy and compassion for others.

Sometimes, if we do bravely open up to someone, we may find that person is so starved for a listening ear that he or she opens a floodgate of woes to share with us. This may not always be a healthy situation, and it can be one more reason why we hesitate to share deeply with other people in the first place. I contend, however, that if the church were living as it should, and every member felt free to express his or her needs in appropriate ways, then individuals would not have to face such overwhelming burdens alone.

Ministry that is separated from real life leaves little appreciable room for understanding what role each family or home plays in it. The scriptures teach that the home is a center of ministry. While church buildings aren't "wrong", they do tend to take away from the need for people to use their homes and other places of contact for ministry. Ministry that occurs outside of the home, generally speaking, is ministry that is out of touch with everyday life. I think this is why there is such an emphasis placed on hospitality in the New Testament. If you want to get to know someone, visit them! Have them over for dinner! It is difficult to know what someone's needs are if we can't see them in everyday life. How many homes from your church have you visited? The scriptures say that we will be known by our love for one another. This kind of love is very difficult to experience in the catacombs of church buildings.

Barrier #2:
Some churches have become ingrown.

Ministry limited to any physical location shifts the attention away from who God has placed in our daily path. Instead, we become focused on what can be done within a certain time frame and location. Over time, the identity of the church becomes its programs. Weary souls visit on Sunday mornings only to leave feeling that they must fit into a mold and are not accepted with open arms. As our programs grow, church becomes something that we get something out of, not something that we give to (beyond our money offerings). Many people have left churches because their "needs" were not met. While the church is a body or household whose design is to meet needs, we forget that this happens as a result of the process of worshipping God and seeking to please Him.

Barrier #3:
Leadership is often not unified on the direction of the church.

Disunity often results when church leaders (such as elders and deacons) see their roles as company managers. So much time is spent fixing the programs that there is very little, or no time, to spend one-on-one with the people of the congregation. The efficiency and results-based protocol of modern business spill over into ministry. The resulting compartmentalization keeps the ministry focused more on the program and less on the hearts of the people. Leadership then becomes "territorial" and divided according to the ministry program. Measurable goals drift from endearing heart-level relationships to numbers-based statistics. Many leadership boards practically fall apart when someone even suggests new ways of "doing church," because they cannot think beyond what they have always done.

Barrier #4:
The church has an unbalanced focus on theology or doctrine.

Theology and doctrine are most important. I would venture to say that most Christians, even the more mature, are confused about what these words mean, or how they apply to life. Christians do need to learn theology and doctrine. The problem, however, is that there is a tendency to focus on inconsequential debates—such as "how many angels can stand on the head of a pin"—rather than learning how the study of doctrine helps develop our relationship with God and others.

I am one who loves to listen to teaching on deep theological and doctrinal issues but often come away thinking, "So what?" Many Christians look at theology and doctrine as something reserved only for the ordained or the very mature. Not so! It is meant for all of us and is a tool for understanding how God wants us to believe and live.

Barrier #5:
Fear often prevents churches from going deeper into the truths of God's Word.

Put another way, many churches suffer because they are a mile wide but only an inch deep. Pastors, elders, deacons, teachers, and others fear offending people and end up soft-peddling God's truth, or not addressing areas of concern at all. Routine sets in. The same messages are heard over and over again: get saved; give money; attend our programs; and witness to your neighbors. Many people secretly long for their church leaders to come out and wrestle with the real-life issues that they grapple with during the week. Leaders avoid personal issues and revealing their own struggles for fear of criticism or loss of respect. As a result, the ministry of the church becomes shallow and irrelevant. Christians become frustrated and unbelievers see no difference between the church and the world. A division occurs between the people who appear to be mature, and the people who are immature and don't understand how to reach maturity. As we reorient our ministry toward tackling the deeper and stickier issues of modern life, we will bring relevancy back to our churches which nurtures the flock and offers hope to the lost.

Barrier #6:
Churches put programs before people.

When the church ceases to be a house of living stones, it can be likened to a monastery. Our churches seem like monasteries when we put programs before people. How can a monastery be attractive to the unbeliever? Good programs that served a useful purpose at one time have become their own self-perpetuating entities. An attitude sets in that says, "We need this program to be healthy," despite the fact that no one wants to lead it or only the same few people bother to attend.

Programs should be seen not just as tools to build maturity but to meet needs. When those needs no longer exist, the program should be re-evaluated, modified or discontinued. We are kidding ourselves when we assume that just because we have a program for everybody that people in our church are growing spiritually. This assumption takes the focus of the church away from faith in Christ and moves it toward faith in our programs. Please understand! Programs are not wrong in and of themselves, but when more time is spent running programs than developing relationships with members of God's family, something may be wrong.

Uniting Together in Purpose on the Foundation

In order to "right" the wrongs that have been done by these worldly notions about church identity and ministry, we need to go back to the foundation of Jesus Christ, who is the corner stone. More specifically, we need to unite together for the purpose of serving God. We must turn aside from the selfishness which turns living stones into lifeless gravel.

We must ask ourselves why God has placed each of us where we are. God has sovereignly ordained each of us to be where we are. Does God call His people together only to divide them, in effect isolating them from each other? Or has He called together a group of people having unique gifts and desires to function in an integrated fashion, resulting in community and purpose?

We are not to become demanding or burdensome in our approach to other people. Rather, we are to commit to serve each other, grow together, confess our sins to each other, and bear one another's burdens in a spirit of unity and love. It is as we seek to glorify God by humbly serving each other that we can begin to see integration take place.

In the same manner that God has sovereignly placed us in our churches, so God has placed each of us in our specific homes, neighborhoods, and communities. As we work at "getting it right" in the church, we will provide a powerful example of how our communities can "get it right". It is not the perfect example, but rather our struggling example which finds resolution in Jesus Christ, that will turn our communities toward the answers found in the Bible. As church life becomes more integrated, it spills over into our communities because life is lived in the "real world" and is not hidden in ecclesiastical fortresses. Furthermore, as lives are changed through in-depth, integrated ministry, we will have newfound zeal for spreading the Good News because we will be able to speak from experience.

Integrated churches with purpose are churches that will build, train, and challenge new believers in a spirit of love. This is what we must learn to do. I believe that God is slowly turning the church toward integrated household ministry. But for this to happen fully, each household must work together with the whole church. The household needs the church and the church needs the household. In the next two chapters, I will investigate the reasons why these two need each other.

We Need Each Other

Part Two

The church needs to learn to produce spiritually mature Christians because we need to stop the failure in many Christian families. More and more children are failing to live their faith and are growing lukewarm toward God and ministry. Some have grown so disgruntled with the disintegration that they even rationalize leaving the local church, refusing to return. Every believer needs the life-giving relationships found only within the church. This chapter will look at nine reasons why families need the church.

"Do We Have To Go To Church?"

c h a p t e r 4

I know of few church-staffers who do not struggle with the following tension in ministry. It seems that very often people, especially children, want to be entertained and have "fun," while the teacher wants to teach them something of value that will enhance their relationship with God. Some will not even attend an event if it offers no entertainment. While I am certainly in favor of having fun, I have always struggled with the apparent conflict that occurs when people expect the gathering of the church to always be entertaining. Are they hungry for fun or hungry for the Lord? I believe that the constant, insatiable thirst for fun often overrides the purposes of the church. This appetite for levity replaces people's true need to learn from men and women who have walked with God and can demonstrate His power in their lives.

People need the church for much more than weekend entertainment. This is particularly true for families. Stable families are the core of our society, providing a safe environment in which to train up children to be the leaders of tomorrow. Today the family is under attack, pulled in every direction. Now more than ever the family needs the church for teaching, modeling, and building up the unique roles that God intended to be the fabric of society. When families turn from—or are no longer a part of—the higher purposes of the church, it is inevitable that societal erosion will result.

I think of a father who feels inept at teaching his children anything because he has not been trained how to teach. Yet this father somehow hopes that another visit to the youth group by a sports hero will strengthen his relationship with his son and help him draw closer to God.

Then there is the teenager who secretly puts up with another sermon on prayer when he has prayed for years, only to have his prayers seemingly go unanswered. Yet he feels he cannot voice his frustrations in church for fear that someone will lecture him with the "party line."

How about the single woman who is wishing that a man in the church would take her son fishing or camping? Or the mother who strongly suspects that her once-committed fourteen-year-old daughter is sleeping around.

Such problems seem to be growing in our society, even in Christian families. I submit that the increasing conflicts we see in our families are strong evidence of the church not meeting their needs.

Our churches are paradoxes in so many ways. They are places where the hurting are supposed to go for comfort, yet they are full of people with no apparent problems. Churches are supposed to be places where we serve God, but they are places where we serve ourselves first. Churches should be places where people can go to be accepted and loved unconditionally, but they are places where it is often hard to "fit in". Churches are places where people should humbly confess and weep over their sins, but they are places where the proud and judgmental meet. Churches should be places where people bond and fellowship on deeper levels, but they are too often places of short, shallow, sound-bite greetings.

The Church Has Failed to Support the Family

The church should be the champion of the family since it is the institution designed by God to nurture and care for families. Despite its many well-intentioned efforts, modern ministry has done very little to help strengthen families. In fact, much ministry has had the opposite effect. Family confusion and dysfunction is as great in Christian families as it is in non-Christian families. Perhaps we can best measure how the church has failed by looking at the future generation. Are youth today ready to take over leadership of the church tomorrow?

Christian Youth Try to Define the Family

In his recent book, *Right from Wrong*, Josh McDowell reports on survey results of 3795 Christian children who were asked a variety of questions concerning their family life and faith.

> A large majority of our youth—three out of every five (60 percent)—buy into the idea of this "nouveau family," defining family as "those who deeply care about you, or whom you deeply care about." Only one in three (32 percent) possess a traditional perspective of what constitutes a family ("people related to each other by birth, adoption, or marriage"). Five percent of our kids say a family is "people living together," and four percent consider "people sharing the same goals or values" to be a family. To put it another way, two-thirds of our kids, when given a choice of four definitions of a "family," select a definition that reflects a "no risk, no commit-

ment" kind of arrangement. Moreover, most of our kids possess a concept of the family that would define cohabiting couples and homosexual unions as a legitimate family; the study indicates that they do not fully realize the implications of their view, but it is there, nonetheless, to shape their reasoning—and their behavior—in the future. (McDowell, p. 62)

How do youth perceive their parents' relationship? "Less than half of our kids (48 percent) say that they want a marriage like that of their parents. Our kids favor divorce by a two-to-one margin for parents who don't love each other" (McDowell, p. 60).

Father-Child Relationship

Regarding time spent with their fathers, 54 percent said that they seldom or never talk to their fathers about personal concerns. Fifty percent responded that they spend anywhere from no time to a grand total of 5-15 minutes each week talking with their fathers about "things that really matter" (McDowell, p. 255). These statistics show a communication gap in the Christian family that is utterly devastating. Christian parents are responsible for modeling Christ to their children and teaching them spiritual truths. How can this be accomplished and children brought to spiritual maturity when children are spending so little time with their fathers?

Morality

Other statistics reveal various forms of sexual impurity and lying as being acceptable. Of 11- to 12-year-olds, 64 percent agree that heavy "French" kissing is acceptable, 26 percent for fondling of breasts, 21 percent for fondling the genitals, and 19 percent for sexual intercourse (McDowell, p. 272). And the percentages go up as the children get older. Many church leaders are scared outright by the dearth of maturity in their youth. In selecting a church, many parents often have a "good" youth group as their number one priority because many are already losing their children to the world and are looking for a safety net.

Truth

Perhaps the most shocking revelation is that 57 percent of the Christian youth in this country do not even know that an objective standard of truth exists (McDowell, p. 15). The impact of this shameful reality cannot be underestimated. Essentially, what this means is that over half of the next generation of Christians feel that they do not need the Bible. Is there a word devastating enough to describe that? This finding also reflects how the moral relativism heaped upon these children every day is clearly winning out over church and parental influence.

Leaving the church

More youth are leaving the church than ever before. Youth programs are having little effect, so says a recent study reported in the April 20, 1996, Washington Times: "In a new study, more than nine in ten congregations report trouble keeping high school students involved." Four in five respondents (youth leaders) reported that it was important for youth to apply their faith to daily life. Of these, only one quarter said that their youth programs were helping them accomplish that goal. The article concludes with what many parents are already discovering: youth want meaningful relationships with adults in the congregation.

What these statistics suggest is that Christian and non-Christian families are crumbling from spiritual neglect. Such households are dysfunctional in equally dysfunctional churches and can no longer communicate across generations. How can a church in this condition expect to provide an effective witness or moral leadership to a wayward country? How can this darkness be lifted when much of the decay has been caused by the once bright light of the church becoming dim...very dim? There are many reasons why the church finds itself in this position. I think one of the greatest is that the church has lost its sense of family and community. The result is that Christianity is viewed, even by some Christians, as a list of do's and don'ts instead of the life-giving web of loving relationships. Without that strong support, our youth have lost the guidance and direction that are intended to come through relationships.

Families need a vibrant, integrated, functional church in which to serve. Lately, many families who feel this lack of integration in their churches have grown disgruntled and now stay home, having decided that they don't need the fellowship of the church. Any family, however, that thinks they don't need Christian fellowship is sorely mistaken. All of God's people—whether individuals, couples, or families—need the church!

Why People Need the Church

I propose the following six reasons why people need the church. (I'm sure there are more.) Let me first define the term "church" as the ministry of believers and not the "organized" church as such.

Reason #1:
People need the church because God says so! (Hebrews 10:25; I Corinthians 12:18-30).

God commands us not to neglect the fellowship of the saints. This alone is reason enough; we are not asked to understand God's commands in order to obey them. Being an active, living, breathing part of the church is essential to our health as individuals and families. We must do as our heavenly Father instructs, knowing that it is His best for us.

Reason #2:
People need the church because it is where they find spiritual protection. (Acts 20:28-31; Hebrews 13:17).

It is the responsibility of church elders to give an account to God for the sheep. As undershepherds of the One Shepherd who laid His life down for the sheep, they are to keep watch over our souls. If we are outside of their influence, we cannot benefit from their protection, and then we become sitting ducks for spiritual attack. Bill Gothard, in his Institute For Basic Life Principles, uses the analogy of an umbrella to illustrate the importance of being under authority. When we are under the umbrella, we stay dry because it shields us from the rain. When we are outside of that protective covering, we are subject to getting drenched. In the same way, the elders of a church serve as a covering. They keep watch for "wolves" that would seek to enter the flock and wreak havoc. They carefully study the scriptures to evaluate current trends or concerns and report to the congregation the issues that could cause harm to individuals and the family.

Reason #3:
People need the church because it is where parents (and other adults) are taught how to model Christ (I Timothy 3:4,5; Titus 2:4-8).

We live in a day when God is turning the hearts of fathers back to their children. Fathers must be taught how to minister effectively to their own children. They must be constantly challenged and encouraged to keep doing so. The failure of fathers to spend time with their wives and children, building those relationships and modeling the ways of Christ before them, is indicative of a broader failure of the church to equip fathers for their vital role in their homes.

The church is also the place where women can be equipped to be godly wives and mothers, learning to keep a balance in their homes among all the demands on their time and attention. The church can help them clarify their priorities and stay focused on the need to teach their children to live godly lives. To accomplish this extraordinary calling, women need the teaching, modeling, support, encouragement, and accountability of older women, who have raised their families and can share the wisdom gleaned from experience. (See Titus 2.)

Both mothers and fathers need clear teaching as to how our society is programming our children to think in ways that are opposed to the Bible and its teachings. The church must instruct all adults how to protect children from the devastating effects of society's withdrawal from God.

Reason #4:
People need the church because it is where families and individuals serve (I Corinthians 12; Acts 16:40).

Families need to serve because they are a microcosm of the church. God's intentions for the church are exemplified within family discipleship. Each household is its own complete society, having its own unique culture. Aspects of government, law, charity, justice, and compassion are inherent to any societal structure and are also found within the family unit. Such components enable households to serve in the most dynamic way. Psalms teaches that God places the lonely in families (Psalm 68:6). Through the church, families come into contact with lonely people and can reach out to them. When families serve individuals in this way, those individuals are strengthened and encouraged to serve others as well.

Reason #5:
People need the church because it is where fellowship can be found (Acts 2:41-47; II Corinthians 6:14-18).

Fellowship in a local body of believers provides accountability, encouragement, and a compass. A compass? Families, if left by themselves, can become isolated and myopic. They need the sharpening afforded by heart-level relationships. This sharpening keeps families "on-purpose" and lessens the possibility that they will wander toward isolation.

What is God doing in our families? Families need to hear how God is working in other families. Just as God deals with the individual, He also deals with the family unit. We hear a lot of sharing from men, women, and sometimes children, but very little sharing from husbands, fathers, wives, and mothers.

Families that isolate themselves from the local body of believers end up being irrelevant to the life of the church and community. Their absence hurts the rest of the body—and themselves. Church relationships provide balance, stability, accountability, and humility. It is prideful to pull out and isolate ourselves. Sometimes we forget that the church is made up of imperfect people and therefore, there can not exist the "perfect" church. Paul warned the Corinthians that they needed each other because they were all parts of the same body. Every part was necessary; no individual part was more important than another. When families isolate themselves, they are basically saying that they are self-sufficient.

A number of the families I work with have grown disgruntled with the status quo, and are grappling with how to respond in a Biblical manner. If you are in such a situation it is my hope that this book will help you make an appeal to your leaders. Take the initiative to help your church make the transition into a more integrated approach to ministry.

Reason #6:

People need the church because it is where they partake of the Lord's Supper (Matthew 5:23, 24; I Corinthians 11:28-32).

Communion (Lord's Supper) is to be celebrated with other members of God's household, not in isolation. Partaking of Communion is a command of God and identifies us with our Savior and His redemptive work. The Biblical communion service has a built-in opportunity for self-examination that helps us to keep short accounts within our own families as well as the larger body of Christ.

Upon review of these six reasons why people need the church, one should keep in mind how life-giving it is to be "in need." We are needy people in that God is our source of strength and guidance every second of every day. He uses relationships in the local church as the primary tool through which He gives us strength and guidance.

In the next chapter I will look more fully at what I mean by an "integrated household approach" to church. As I have discussed in this chapter, families need the church, and the church needs strong families. When referring to families, I mean to include all the other households that make up the church—single men, women, couples without children, as well as families with growing children. The church needs all of these various households, relating in healthy ways to one another. In the next chapter, I will look at how the strength of church ministry depends upon households.

In the same way that the people need the church, the church also needs its leaders. An integrated approach to ministry allows for ministry to be an all-involving process, not something that is simply for the ordained. Chapter five examines what an integrated church ministry looks like.

"What Do They Want Now...?"

c h a p t e r 5

Since the time of Moses, there have been instances of friction between church leaders and the congregation. No aspect of the church and its ministry is immune to the scrutiny of its members. Members can get frustrated when they feel that their concerns fall upon deaf ears. Being in a leadership position myself, I assure you, there are some reciprocal tensions.

I think of the pastor who is always on the run, drained by the demands of the congregation. He takes phone calls at all hours of the night trying to mediate explosive situations and patch up tearing relationships. There is no apparent end to this cycle. One crisis is defused only to be followed by another.

Then there is the elder who is wrestling with budget limitations and fuming about a congregation that wants more but is not willing to sacrifice and help to get more.

The church's deacons often serve unusual hours, giving of their free time to perform largely unseen, thankless jobs. The joy of serving slowly becomes a struggle to maintain a good attitude when people complain about how the job is done.

How about the youth leader or children's pastor who pours his guts out working long hours (for little pay) thinking up ways to generate some glimmer of spiritual acumen in the children? More often than not, the youth leader leaves these carefully planned activities believing himself to be a glorified baby-sitter. Week after week, year after year, the children show little growth and look more and more like their worldly counterparts. This hard work means very little to those parents who expect the church to straighten out their children for them.

Oddly, the area of music is one of the most volatile areas of potential conflict. Many choir directors work hard to put together a well thought out selection of songs to be sung on a Sunday morning only to have a few "sour notes" in the congregation complain about length, style, or the pace at which they are sung.

A common trait that these leaders share is the toll that ministry often takes on their own families. Something has to give among these demands, and too often it is their own family life that suffers.

The joys that come with being a church leader are not without frustration, discouragement, and temptations to give up. What often compounds these emotions is the leader's attempt to do all the work himself.

Attitudes sometime develop toward volunteers as a staff member thinks to himself, "He isn't the professional, I am. If he does the job, it will surely get messed up, and I'll look like I'm shirking responsibility and not doing my job." Or, "If someone else does it, I'll lose control of the ministry." "If they don't like the way I do it, then they can leave." "No one has ever offered to help out. They're lazy and don't care anyway."

Leaders who have these attitudes are, in effect, planting seeds of division and disintegration. Such attitudes indicate a lack of meaningful, creative involvement of individuals and families in ministry vision, planning, and implementation. I believe that there is a better way.

Getting the work of the church done needs to be looked at differently. We need to think in a way that integrates individuals. Instead of a one-man show, ministry should be a cast of many characters. How can leaders overcome these heartrending attitudes and be free to serve God, not a bureaucracy?

The place to begin is with the development and exposition of a fresh vision.

Without Vision, the People Perish

The demands of sustaining multiple church activities often obscures the vision of church leaders. It is easy, therefore, to see how a church's identity can stray from being a place for meaningful relationships to a hub of disintegrated activities. If we try to force integrated vision into existing programs and activities, we will meet with resistance. Reversing this trend will require a great deal of patience and love on the part of leaders. Now let us look at how this trend can be reversed.

Vision begins to collapse when the leaders see themselves as the ones doing all the work. Ministry is to be done by the entire body of Christ, not only the paid staff. Ministry is everybody's business. If you bear the name of Christ, you are a minister. We are all living stones.

Still, most people do not think of themselves as "ministers." There could be several reasons for this. One reason is that we have grown up with this wrong idea of the church (as covered in chapter two) which has brought with it a division that implies that the leaders are to serve while the members are to be served. Another reason is that the church has been so institutionalized it is more similar in dynamic to a business operating in a top-down manner through managers, than the "household of households" it was destined to be.

Leaders must begin to see themselves as leaders. They lead other leaders, they are doers, but they are not solo performers. Part of the job of a leader is to imbibe himself and the congregation in a vision. They must share this vision through their words, priorities, and lives. They must motivate people to participate in this process in order to stimulate other parts of the body of Christ that have atrophied from lack of use. The unique perspective of each person can help sharpen the overall vision and give it new life.

The body must have a role in cultivating the vision. This can be rather scary. I know from personal experience. When you have done something a certain way for many years, you become comfortable with it. The thought of changing the way you've always done something can be paralyzing even if you know the benefits will be freeing and rewarding. Many businesses fear change, or expanding into new markets with new products, so they cut off dialog before it gets started. The result is that they don't reach their full potential. In the same way, churches that are heavy with top-down approaches to ministry—approaches that essentially tell others what to do, or leave them out of the doing altogether—smash the creative and gifted living stones.

Some of these ideas may seem unusual or light-years ahead, but listening to people's thoughts through the hearing aid of their gifts and abilities gives them ownership of the vision and a commitment to pursue it. They have made a contribution to a much larger goal. They see where they fit in and that they are important participants. In summary, they affect the outcome.

It can be stifling to serve where someone else has already locked down every detail of the vision, as well as exactly how ministry will be done. This situation binds people's creativity and ability to exercise their spiritual gifts. A person who is not totally immersed and sold on the ministry can become stale and lifeless instead of life-giving.

As we bring people back into ministry, we must be patient with them. People take a while to understand an idea, let alone embrace it and begin to live it out. It requires great patience to cultivate people this way. We are working with the serious handicaps of church tradition and hectic lifestyles which have conditioned people to be complacent and uninvolved. People must first see that they have a meaningful contribution before they can feel comfortable participating. Only then will they embrace a vision for remodeling their church life toward an integrated household approach to ministry.

What Is the Vision of an Integrated Household Ministry?

How does an integrated household ministry look? How does it work? Believe it or not, an integrated household ministry is easier to operate, and more effective in the long run, than common traditional church. There are several key aspects to an integrated household ministry:

1. An integrated household ministry looks like a family because it is actually a family of families.

To begin with, the family, or household, is a model of integration at its best. This truth is clear in the scriptures from Genesis to Revelation. God uses "household" terminology to reveal how the church is to function. As previously mentioned, a household includes not only the nuclear family—Dad, Mom, and kids—but also singles, single-parent families, and all of the other individuals present in the body of Christ. Please be reminded that when I use the term "household" in this integrated approach to ministry, I in no way intend to shortchange those who don't belong to a "typical" household. Individuals still have identity and are vital parts of church ministry, only they now have an integrated structure within which to participate. Their influence extends beyond a segregated group into various age and interest strata.

2. An integrated ministry has a primary focus on equipping parents as leaders of households.

In Ephesians, chapter five, fathers are commanded to be the leaders of their families. They must love and cherish their wives as they would their own bodies, and teach their children with love and patience. Mothers are the strategic helpers of the fathers, and in cases where there is no father or the father is not a Christian, she fills the role of primary spiritual leader. If parents are to take what is taught at church and apply it to their everyday lives, they need to be involved in the planning process. Only then can parents take ownership of the church's vision and its outworking, and are committed to seeing it succeed. They also share responsibility for others in their households, such as singles. These are some of the ways parents are ministry leaders.

Elders and their wives work with fathers and mothers both together and individually to provide challenge, encouragement, and accountability. This form of discipleship simplifies ministry since the focus placed on fathers and the mothers who, in turn, minister to their own households. **In effect, the leadership begins to work through fathers and mothers instead of working around them.**

Heads of households become close friends with the leaders as they work, plan, and grow side by side. Leaders can then be assured that what is taught at church is being understood and implemented in each home. This focus is crucial if the church is going to rebuild family life and strengthen future generations.

This is where the church has dropped the ball in the past. We must pick it back up. We must equip parents for spiritual leadership in the home.

3. An integrated ministry uses heart-level relationships as its primary method for ministry.

Jesus Christ died for us so we could have a heart-level relationship with our Creator. God's working in us, strengthening our relationship with Him, is what our lives are about. It is this primary relationship that sets the tone for our relationships with other people. The two "great" commandments and the Sermon on the Mount further reveal the priority God places on the heart. An integrated ministry uses heart-level relationships as its primary method for ministry because they are most effective. Think of heart-level relationships as the fiber from which the quilt of home and church integration is made.

4. In an integrated ministry, everyday life becomes the theater in which heart-level relationships are played out.

Programs, especially those that center on the church building, take a back seat to relationships. Ask yourselves, "Is what we are doing building spiritual maturity in relationships?" "Is it fostering people reaching out to each other beyond Sunday morning, or is it a once-a-week gig?" **Programs should serve the purpose of building personal, discipleship-oriented relationships, not replace them.**

Older men working with younger men and older women working with younger women is the prescription for relationships within the church. Within a family context, this means fathers and mothers discipling their children.

Singles and single-parent families can be "adopted" by traditional families. Being a part of a family unit helps to ensure that these individuals are consistently loved, taught, and equipped in a framework. Personal discipleship-oriented relationships within these adapted households strengthens individuals to overcome habitual sin, thus breaking the bondage of generational sin. In such an environment, singles who never had a Christian role model, or divorced single parents and their children, are kept safe and nurtured until they mature enough to provide spiritual leadership in their own households. Mark Hayes' experience (as related in chapter one) is but one example which testifies to the effectiveness of household ministries to singles.

5. An integrated church is one where the family unit is a dynamic witness to neighbors and communities.

Family members serving together as a unit sends a message to the world that the gospel of Jesus Christ is powerful to restore and keep families together. It is ironic that men and women who are proficient at solving multitudes of technical problems at work often struggle to solve common problems that exist in their own family relationships. Integrated churches are reaching generations of unbelievers who have "heard" the gospel but never actually "seen" it lived out. These days, just seeing a family together in day-to-day harmony is a tremendous witness that often evokes questions such as "Why are your children so well-behaved?" or "Your family does so much together, why?" These are the questions that often lead to verbal gospel presentations. Seeing a family together in harmony is one of the best ways to reach our neighborhoods and communities that have written off Christianity as having solutions to their problems.

6. An integrated ministry frees people to minister where they are.

Integrated ministry centers on family life, not the church building, so people are not bound by program schedules or bureaucracy. Our neighborhoods and communities need to be sprinkled with salt. This means we must turn the saltshaker upside down! Relationships make it possible to develop ministry anywhere and at any time, whether in the store, library, or a neighbor's house. The salt flavors and preserves wherever it falls. Everyone has experienced the frustration of a clogged saltshaker! Well, this illustrates what happens when we relegate ministry to programs that exist primarily within the four walls of the church. This clogs many outlets for ministry.

7. An integrated church sees responsibility to its neighbors as much more than presenting a "canned" outline of the gospel.

Until recently, the church has historically played an enormous role in the community. It was the place where the hungry were fed and naked clothed. Widows and orphans were cared for by churches. Doing these things is as much a presentation of the gospel as the "Romans Road", "The Four Spiritual Laws", or "Evangelism Explosion". In an integrated ministry, households are encouraged to carry out these ministries socially, in their homes and neighborhoods. However, this is dramatically different from the Social Gospel or "Do-Gooderism"; this is loving your neighbor as yourself.

8. The heart-level relationships which form the integrated church enable people the freedom to get help for their deepest, "darkest" secrets.

This church is one where people are accepted, rags and all, and loved unconditionally. However, when ministry is divided up, it is very easy to fall into a mindset where people know what is accepted and only perform to that level. In such a situation, the focus is on earning our place, or fitting in, rather than full acceptance.

9. An integrated church is one where people derive great benefit from serving, rather than receiving.

The un-integrated church is often built around meeting people's felt needs by catering to their selfish desires. While meeting needs is a part of the church, this is not the whole picture. We do need our legitimate needs met, but we are also to seek to meet the needs of others. In an integrated format, people find that many of their deepest needs are met by God through relationships, instead of church programs. It is through serving others that we often find our needs diminish, or go away altogether, because our focus is taken off of ourselves.

One of the most important aspects of an integrated ministry is that the pastor and leadership are able to enjoy ministry more fully. This is because they are free from the "tyranny of the urgent", a zillion activities, useless meetings, and emergencies. They can focus on prayer, reading and studying the Word, and challenging the other leaders of the church and households.

I have to be honest and say that an integrated approach is not the approach to use if one is gunning for fast church growth. So far, it has produced numbers, but it has not produced huge numbers because life-changing heart-level relationships require months, sometimes years to produce such outward measures of fruit. The numbers, however, that it has produced have been genuine as opposed to the many "tares" that are harvested with other approaches. **Consider further that far too many pews are filled with Christians who remain spiritual infants because after they were "won to Christ," were left to disciple themselves.**

Pastor Ben Taylor is building ministry through household relationships and recently told me about a family in his church whose thirteen-year-old son did not want to come on Sunday morning or participate in any spiritual activities. The method the parents employed in trying to deal with him was to use strict, regimented discipline. When the son would not go to church, they went to the point of disconnecting the power to the house so that he couldn't play Nintendo while his family was gone. The parents came to Ben one night expressing their desire to go to a church with a youth group. Ben counseled the parents to consider that they were not loving their son and because of this, a youth group would do little for them. Apparently, they were just counting the days until he turned eighteen and could leave the house. "It really sounds like you are actually hating your son. You're just wanting him to be fixed so that the family will be better," Ben said. He talked to the father about how to love his son, spending time, interacting in his son's world. As the father began to show love to his son, his son began to take it to heart. Father and son started mowing the grass and doing other church activities together. The father really began to spend time with him. The boy's heart changed. Now sixteen, he is active in church, loves the Lord, and the whole family is very close-knit. Heart-level relationships that are bathed in the love of Christ are enormous tools for building maturity.

Are you beginning to get the picture? An integrated household approach to ministry focuses on relationships in a way that a program-based ministry cannot. Relationships, learning to love one another, are what Christianity is truly all about! Let's move deeper now into our discussion of the church as a household of households.

A Renewed Vision For The Church And Its Ministry

Part Three

The church is far more than a collection of individuals, families, and programs. The church is described many ways in scripture: a body, the bride of Christ, an army, and a household...God's household. The image of church as God's household opens up a plethora of truths about who we are, how we relate to one another, and how we reach the world with the gospel. We will rediscover these timeless truths and see how applying them will not only build ministry relationships, but also provide a major octane boost to outreach.

Back To The DrawingBoard: The Church Is An Extented Household

chapter 6

We have seen that pastors and laypeople alike feel a sense of disconnection between church and everyday life. This disconnection is increased by the transient nature of life and work as well as the general brokenness of homes today.

One recent answer has been to "restore the household." But often this has been an effort from outside the church, apart from the vision and life of the church. We have specialized men's, women's, and youth ministries today that "reach" or "minister to the needs of" these groups. In this, we are allowing parachurch groups to do the work the church is not doing. Sunday morning is set aside for doctrinal training and sermons that sometimes address only a limited range of human needs.

Could our many needs and problems be better addressed, better resolved, by bringing more of the traditionally church-specific jobs into the home? (Such as, reinforcing doctrine, morals, etc.) And by bringing more of our household and life-related struggles under the guidance of the church? Instead of the compartmentalization of life, which many of us now experience, suppose we integrated church and home?

How would we envision the church differently if we wanted to integrate church and home? Do we see how important it is to do so—given that households are the front-line forces that are challenged in everyday life by the world's ills and needs?

What would have to change in our church curricula and our approach to home fellowship?

Before we look thoroughly at what would have to change in our curricula and approaches, we need to think through the vision. Having seen the need today...how do we see ourselves, the church, as a distributor of God's solutions to help a fallen, broken, isolated, and struggling world? This is urgent because vision is the foundation for all we do now and all we will do in the future.

What Is the Church?

In the scriptures, the church is described in several ways. It is the body of Christ, the bride of Christ, an army, and God's household. Together, all of these and other descriptions are components of the church's identity. These seemingly diverse descriptions are like the many prisms of colored light that bounce into your eye through a perfect diamond. Each ray is beautiful—gloriously beautiful—and gives us a deeper appreciation for the church.

The church is a body. Paul uses the body analogy in 1 Corinthians 12 to communicate the importance of each spiritual gift to the church. Each Christian has a unique role to play in the life of the church. This view is the most widely known and has become the basis for involvement in various programs. (Though we are not always good at caring for our busy workers when they burn out—or preventing such burn out in the first place. Many of the gifts people have do not fit into our programmatic systems!) **Perhaps the reason that so many people struggle with their spiritual gifts is that ministry has been confined within the sterile walls of a church building and has not been carried out enough in homes and the milieu of daily life.** I would submit that many people's gifts are rendered useless to the body because they are not seen as useful in the limited confines of a church building!

The church is the bride of Christ. Ephesians 5:22-32 uses the marriage relationship that exists between Christ (the bridegroom) and His church (the bride) to describe how husbands and wives ought to relate with each other. The Song of Solomon provides an analogy for the depth and intimacy of relationship that God desires to have with His church. This view has much to offer the church in terms of our relationships with each other.

The church is an army. The fleshly wars between God's people and God's enemies we read about in the Old Testament provide a mental image of what is true for Christians today. We are soldiers (1 Tim. 2:3) on an invisible battlefield fighting an invisible enemy (Eph. 6:10-20). This view has helped to mobilize Christians in prayer, political, and social action for which we are slowly regaining a positive reputation in the public square.

The church is God's household. Except for marquees and bulletin covers, this view has been practically divorced from the everyday life of the church. The pervasive influence of individualism has infected the church to such an extent that we have a difficult time understanding the church as a household to any practical degree.

What could result if we wiped the dust off this view, examined it very closely, and began to evaluate church vision and ministry according to it?

The identity of the church as God's household is pervasive in scripture. God's identity is that of a "Father": our "heavenly

Father" (Matthew 5:48), "Abba, father"—which means "Daddy" (Romans 8:15). Jesus is God's "Son," the "first-born of many brethren." Christians are God's "children" (Romans 8:12); God's "sons" (v. 14), who are "adopted" (vv. 15, 23), and who are "joint heirs" with Christ (v. 17). Jesus is the "husband" and the church is His bride (Eph. 5:23). The church is God's household (Acts 13:26).

Notice also how the names of God that reflect His role in our relationship also reflect the relationship fathers have with their households. Some of these names include: "protector" (Psalm 121:7); "provider" (Genesis 22:14); and "leader" (Exodus 13:3).

The late nineteenth-century pastor, B.M. Palmer, wrote extensively about the church's identity as a "household." In his book, *The Family*, he writes,

> These [household statements] are so numerous as to require a skillful classification, in order to bring them all under review. And when the more direct testimonies have been recited, there will remain a large body of scripture, in which the general idea is interwoven into the whole texture of the language. It is one of the evidences of inspiration that the great doctrines of grace are conveyed to such an extent by implication. So that, if a destructive criticism should succeed in blotting out the formal and explicit statements of Christian doctrine, it would be found so thoroughly incorporated in other passages that, *the entire web of scripture language must be torn to shreds before the truth could be eliminated* [emphasis mine]. This is just one of those marvelous expedients of Divine wisdom which brings to naught all the subtlety of human exposition, when it undertakes the sad work of obliterating the record which God has

given of Himself. (Palmer, p. 264)

Not only is the church a household, it is "the fundamental idea of the church" (Palmer, p. 209). There are many evidences of this apparent truth. I will focus on two that Palmer raises: (1) Features of the household are reproduced in the church, and (2) The primary place for ministry is the home.

Features of the Household are Reproduced in the Church

Palmer describes two of the most essential features that prove the church's identity as a household.

Fellowship

The first, he states, is that of fellowship.

The fellowship of the family does not found upon mere association, nor simply upon community of interest, as in society at large; but upon community of origin, upon natural relationship, and upon instinctive affection. It is one of blood, and a common life pervades the whole. (Palmer, p. 268)

One's son or daughter from childhood through adulthood, including marriage, is always the son or daughter of their parents.

The church is the same way.

There is a prevailing harmony, which the utmost perverseness can scarcely destroy, springing out of this oneness of origin. All bear the same name as their signature; all live upon the same bounty, and are sheltered by the same providence; all obey the same authority, are molded by the same discipline, and are at last heirs to the same possessions; while through all these interests runs the electric current of an instinctive affection, making each member a partaker of one common family life. (Palmer, pp. 269-70)

Thus no other institution exists wherein many different people can be eternally joined together. Many rulers of history have sought in vain to divide, silence, even destroy this great household, but to no avail. What binds us together is not man-made, but written in the blood of the Most High God. The old adage to describe household relationships applies to the church: "Blood is thicker than water."

Discipline

Discipline, a major element in the life of a child, is part of the Christian life.

> It is for discipline that you endure; God deals with you as sons; for what son is there whom his father does not discipline? But if you are without discipline, of which all have become partakers, then you are illegitimate children and not sons. Furthermore, we had earthly fathers discipline us, and we respected them; shall we not much rather be subject to the Father of spirits, and live? For they disciplined us for a short time as seemed best to them, but He disciplines us for our good, that we may share in His holiness. All discipline for the moment seems not to be joyful, but sorrowful; yet to those who have been trained by it, afterwards it yields the peaceful fruit of righteousness. (Hebrews 12:7-12)

Just as our heavenly Father disciplines us with love, so we are to discipline our children in love and the church is to discipline unrepentant believers in love. Could it be that the failure of many churches to practice discipline within the body (Matthew 18) is a reflection of fathers and mothers not disciplining their sons and daughters in the home? This failure creates generational cycles of churches and homes who know not the blessings of restoration which follow discipline and forgiveness.

The Church Finds Its Home in the Household

As we trace the history of the church beginning in Adam to the New Testament, we see that household relationships were often key contributors to the church. In Jesus' ministry this theme continues. Many of Jesus' miracles and teaching were performed in homes. After Pentecost, we see the people of God gathering not as individuals but as households. Notice that after Peter's first sermon, the people of the church were "breaking bread from house to house, they were taking their meals together with gladness and sincerity of heart" (Acts 2:46). Christians were under persecution, which made meeting in homes necessary. But clearly, the church prospered in the home. The church grew exponentially during this period of history.

A survey through the New Testament reinforces the household as the basis of the church: Mary (Acts 12:12); Aquila and Priscilla (Acts 18:2); Chloe (1 Corinthians 1:11); Stephanus (1 Corinthians 16:15); Onesiphorus (2 Timothy 1:16); and Nympha (Colossians 4:15). "Under the New Testament economy, where the Church assumes her final form, the family is again her home" (Palmer, p. 207).

Note that the kind of individual identity that we see in our multitudinous age-segregated programs has no place in the history of the church until recently. These programs have done very little to contribute to the long-term effectiveness of the gospel and spiritual maturity.

The Household Is a Redemptive Unit

Paul encouraged young widows to be remarried in 1 Timothy 5:11. This point stresses the importance of women not being alone but either living in the state of marriage or under the protective roof of another household. This was to be accomplished in households adopting these individuals. The household is thus a redemptive unit, not just a place where children are raised up in the fear and admonition of the Lord. It is the place where other individuals are protected from the tragedies of life and through nurture and love are discipled to return to meaningful service. Ministry to orphans and widows was of special concern to God as He restates this concern as a priority in James 1:27. "This is pure and undefiled religion in the sight of our God and Father, to visit orphans and widows in their distress, and to keep oneself unstained by the world."

Characteristics of Early Church Household Life

In a day when many parents seek to get away from their children, we see in contrast that God's standard was for the household to worship and serve together as a unit, not as individuals.

There are several examples of this principle in scripture. One such example is in the book of Exodus where we read that the Passover was to be enjoyed as a household. Those households that could not eat a whole lamb were to eat the meal with another household (Exodus 12:4). This tradition continued throughout Israel's history. Other religious festivals that marked the Jewish calendar were household events as well. Christians are instructed to continue to join together in the celebration of communion.

The Early Church Shared Possessions

The early church was so enthralled by the work of God that they voluntarily gave up their possessions in order to benefit the needs of their brothers and sisters in Christ. The church appears to have come a long way from that practice. I recently heard about a church that turned down a request for funds by one of its members (a single mother). The leaders told her to go get a welfare check. "After all, this is what we pay taxes for!" they later explained when questioned. I submit that church is sinning by abdicating the care of its members to the federal and state governments.

Biblically, the care of orphans, widows, and those less fortunate is the responsibility of the church, not the government. The government takes more and more authority—and consequently, freedom—away from the household as we sit transfixed in complacency. It has been a known and accepted responsibility of the household to take care of its own, not just for Christians but for non-Christians as well. It was not until 1935 that the Social Security Act usurped the household of its care-giving role and shifted responsibility to the government. This can change, but households must wake up and take back the responsibility. When bills cannot be paid, when a house is burned down, when the only car a household has will not run, when a father is out of work and cannot afford groceries, when unexpected medical bills are enormous, the church must step in and meet that need. I particularly have been blessed by my church's application of this principle. When my wife and I lost our first daughter—on Christmas Day, tragically—the leaders quickly provided financial assistance, helping to pay the humongous bills that we incurred.

They Were of "One Mind"

These were households who truly bore one another's burdens with a love that would not fade or turn away to the idol of convenience. With everybody divided into little groups that seldom interact one must wonder if the church today is unified. Our current methods are too divisive for these things to happen on a regular, meaningful level. Being of one mind requires some degree of togetherness.

What Is a Household?

The whole concept of household has been perverted today by our individualized society. Therefore, I thought it helpful to bring us back to some basic ideas of what a household is supposed to be and do. The church cannot be the extended household that God intended if we try to build upon a false understanding.

A household supports the needs and spiritual growth of the individual so that the individual can mature and in turn support the needs and growth of others. Each person helps the others while being helped themselves. Everyone from the youngest children to the oldest grandparents can contribute to household life to some degree. The young child who receives help and nurture will one day grow up to be a primary nurturer himself, thus starting the process all over again! Quite a worthwhile investment indeed!

A household is more than a structure for simply carrying out day-to-day tasks and responsibilities. If it were just a prescription for "who does what" and was void of deep and caring relationships, it would make for a pretty boring, stale, and sad life.

The household should be a structure of meaningful relationships, not an assembly line of menial tasks and duties. If, instead, we look at roles and responsibilities through relationships, they become a means to an end—loving, nurturing, and building multi-generational fruit—not an end in themselves. It is as easy to see the spirit of emptiness, isolation, and devastation in a weak or abusive household, as it is to see the spirit of fullness, joy, and friendship in a healthy household. The same is true for churches.

Today we see many churches whose structure is set up to support many ministries and activities, not necessarily the health and growth of its members. For instance, rule keeping and debates on "gray" issues, various evangelical works, activities, mission trips, and teaching can and often do supersede relationships. In some cases, if we simply took the time to equip new people, instead of always doing the work the same way with the same tired people, we would find the work done far more effectively.

The life-blood of relationships in the household and the church is love. Love is behind the strength, health, and connectedness of relationships. In Matthew 22:37-40, Jesus told His disciples that the greatest two commandments were to love God and love our neighbor. He went even further to say that the whole law and the prophets is based on the above definition of love. Paul, in 1 Corinthians 13:13, clearly states that the greatest of all gifts is love! Again in Galatians 5:13 Paul exhorts the believers to serve one another through love. In the book of 1 John, we learn that if we do not love our brother but say we love God, we really do not love God!

Finally, a household is inclusive in two ways. First, a household consists of all its members. Although each person has a different role, responsibility, and level of authority, each is equal in their importance. Each household member—no matter what his/her role—should put aside his/her own desires to serve the other(s) out of love. For instance, a father may decide to put aside his own hobbies and interests to care for a wife who is seriously ill, or give up a night at chess club just to spend time with his son or daughter.

God's design for churches is that His children are included and connected because they are integrated into the life—not necessarily the organization—of the church. They have an important role that makes them indispensable to others. In some churches where people are not integrated in love, fragmentation and isolation occurs, and the deeper needs of people stay hidden within them. Love is what is needed for people to totally open up and share their deepest concerns and secrets.

The second way that a household is inclusive is that it includes others who are outside of it. I remember as a child addressing household friends as "Aunt" or "Uncle." We would visit them and they would visit us. We would share many fantastic memories. This designation didn't even faze me until I was much older and I realized that neither of my parents had any brothers or sisters! How come I had been calling people "Aunt" and "Uncle" when I did not have any? In life and death, they were looked at by me and my siblings as household members (even though there was no blood relation).

We all seek those close friends who share in our happiness, sadness, and personal needs—those with whom we can be completely transparent. These people become absorbed into our households and have great potential for enriching our lives. They give us counsel and are "there" when we need them the most. We in turn let them into our hearts and lives. We respect them. When others sense that they are needed on such an elemental level they develop a deeper sense of worth and dignity. They see that they are valuable to others.

Imagine what rediscovering just these simple aspects of what a household is would do for the church household. Imagine further what shining this light on churches could do for the life of the church both inside and outside of our fellowship circles. A love that spawns deep heart-level connectedness that transcends the organization as described above will strengthen not just the church but its effect on an increasingly lonely, isolated, and directionless world.

I believe that this vision of the church as a household of households is absolutely crucial to our effectiveness in the world for Christ. Our churches are full of broken, near broken, and partially rebuilt people. Of concern is that these people are not connecting with many of our programs and getting the help they need. For instance, the needs of a fourteen-year-old boy from a broken home may not be helped by the youth program. This boy does not need to attend another game day or sit in a Bible study taught by a young, idealistic youth leader. An older, more mature man is much more qualified to help by sitting, listening, teaching, modeling, and loving. This relationship builds the trust that is necessary to get to the heart issues that can best be addressed with seasoned wisdom and an example of what the Christian life is supposed to be.

Ministry through relationship involves letting the individual know that we are here for the long haul—that we will not forsake them, or ostracize them because they reveal some shameful secret. God's model for us is specific, "There is therefore now no condemnation for those who are in Christ Jesus" (Romans 8:1). If we have the mind of Christ, then we must include this model. People must be sure that they are loved before they will open up the heavy iron door that guards their hearts. Just attending a class will not provide what's necessary to get to the real issues in one's life. It will also affect our present ministry by leading the church back to common, unified vision within local bodies. A common vision remedies the splintered and competing nature of multitudinous programs and the "organization" by unifying the body in spirit, purpose, and love.

In the future, this vision will produce multigenerational fruit. So much church ministry accommodates the repetitive cycle of failure. I would go so far as to say that we expect failure and therefore accommodate it. **Many of our ministries remain**

in a kind of self-inflicted exile, helping the constant, fundamental failures of Christians. This becomes our focus, and we never seem to rise above patching things up. If churches re-catch the household vision, instead of the next generation having to start over, a generation will rise up that has been trained in righteousness and will live it out.

Going back to the example of the fourteen-year-old youth...if past is prologue to the future, we should not be surprised when the fourteen-year-old repeats the failure of his own parents and comes back several years later for counseling after going through a messy divorce. How can we expect otherwise? Has he seen an example, or been in contact with one who is of greater maturity, or has walked in his shoes? Under a renewed vision, this fourteen-year-old would be included in household life so that he can see how it functions and get a vision for a bright future. Ten years later, he can then lead other troubled teens into a haven of acceptance, love, and purpose, instead of being yet another casualty.

Our Greatest Impact Is Through Relationships

We cannot forget that the greatest effects on peoples' lives are made through relationships. It is through relationships that we can best help a person grow into a loving, caring, and equipped Christian.

God uses household terminology to emphasize the quality and enduring nature of relationships within His household. New Christians are called "babes" and need the intensive care that a human baby would need (1 Peter 2:2). Maturing Christians are referred to as "children": "Brethren, do not be children in your thinking; yet in evil be babes, but in your thinking be mature" (1 Corinthians 14:20). Mature men are referred to as "fathers" and younger men as "brothers": "Do not rebuke an older man but rather appeal to him as a father, to the younger men as brothers" (1 Timothy 5:1). Older women are referred to as "mothers" and younger women as "sisters": "the older women as mothers, and the younger women as sisters" (1 Timothy 5:2).

When the church discovers it is a household, it will affect individuals in the church in the following ways. First, children. Children play an active role in the life of the church—especially when they themselves are ministering within the context of their household. Children (as an age-segregated group) have little to offer an adult world other than a responsibility to be served and be shown a fun time. Granted, the role of a child is not as complex as that of an adult, but it is no less important. Indeed, children serving in ministry with their parents can be a tremendous asset to the church. Because children spend more time serving with their parents, they can mature faster mentally, emotionally, and spiritually. Helping out in small, maybe unseen ways helps them learn humility and the importance of small things. They develop a vision for what the Christian life and church life are supposed to be. They are more challenged to be involved in serving others.

Second, young adults. Young adults are affected the same as the children mentioned above. The key here, though, is that young people from early high school through college are even more in need of the maturity and counsel afforded through the connectedness with those who have the wisdom to help them. This is a time of making decisions about vocation, marriage, and financial management. Young people need just as much, or even more training than adults. With today"s youth subculture reaching its cagey claws toward our youth constantly, the need is even greater to be involved in both household and church household life. Being older, they can involve themselves in a broader range of responsible ministry—ministry that challenges them to a higher moral standard.

Third, other adults whether they are couples, singles, single-parent households, divorced, widowed, etc. can all be greatly helped by this exciting format for ministry. Our ultimate spiritual goals are best met in relationships. The politics of labels ironically designed to help the individual has in fact done the individual harm. It sets up barriers to relationships by pointing out what is different about a person, not what is similar. It is difficult here to explain fully how the psychology of labels has hurt human relationships. Unfortunately, the church has only become a reflection of this labeling. Suffice it to say, it has damaged the household atmosphere of connectedness, love, and commitment by limiting people to fellowshipping with those who are alike. The vision of a household-based church makes it possible for these individuals, even those whose redeemed lives are still marked by the scars of sin, to be accepted and loved. The "household" is the first and best approach to dealing with the unique needs of the individual.

Discovering the church as a household will impress people outside our churches because they see Christians loving and serving each other. They will not have to wait to hear the "Romans Road", "The Four Spiritual Laws", or "Evangelism Explosion". They will see it with their eyes and hear it with their ears! They will say, "Wow!"

I am reminded of a man in our church who built an addition onto his house with the constant volunteer help of others in the church. His next-door neighbor made a profession of faith after seeing this outpouring of love on behalf of the brothers. No canned gospel presentation could do what that living example did! I am also reminded of a single woman who made a profession of faith upon being visited by a father and son. She told me that because the son was with his father, honoring him, proved to her that the faith to which they gave testimony was true. God used that visit—not a flawless explanation of the gospel—to bring her to the point of making a profession of faith.

Growth

As a husband, father, and ministry leader, my primary goal is to influence the spiritual growth of those around me. Just as children grow up physically, so too are Christians to grow up spiritually. Spiritual growth is beautiful and fulfilling. It is the only thing that matters once we die and go on to be with the Lord.

As parents delight in the growth of their children, so are spiritual parents to delight in the spiritual growth of their spiritual children. "I have no greater joy than this, to hear of my children walking in the truth" (3 John 4).

Household names and relationships are like parables to the church, describing how God deals with His people and how His people are to deal with each other. The question must be raised, what is the effect upon the church when these connections are not made in the life of the church? More specifically, how will a boy or a girl mature in his walk with God if he does not first experience loving discipline in the home from his own parents? How will a boy rise to becoming an overseer in the church if he grows up in a home that is governed by chaos and devoid of leadership? How will boys and girls practice love and service in the household of God if they do not grow up practicing it within their households? Most of all, what kind of understanding will a child have of God the Father, if that child only spends twenty minutes a week in meaningful conversation with his dad?

Even though God in His grace continues to prove faithful, working through man's failure to live in concert with His revealed plan, why should we presume upon His grace? Why shouldn't we strive for His best for us? Why shouldn't we try to mirror these relationships and make the connections between household and church?

I will close this chapter by emphasizing a very important point about this renewed vision. Although I have already alluded to it, it bears repeating. I believe that through this vision, we can have an unprecedented impact upon our world for Christ. The Church of the Lord Jesus Christ could have an impact on the world that has not been seen for at least a hundred years, if not more. We do not want to see this renewed vision turn in on itself. As my good friend, Stewart Jordan, says, "it must be about accomplishing the Great Commission." Following is one way that I believe we can do just that.

Before Social Security and LBJ's "Great Society" programs, the churches were the primary assistance-givers to the poor. We stand to make quite an effect upon our society for God and bring Him great glory if we could serve these people using biblical welfare principles. **In this way, the integration of the church and household model can do what the government can never do, which is minister to their heart.**

Newspapers are offering more and more articles and editorials about churches picking up the ball in this area. A July 13, 1995, Metropolitan Times insert featured on the front page, "A Helping Hand: Churches May Adopt Welfare Families." In her column titled, "Needed: Welfare Reform in the Nation's Churches" of the May 16, 1996, Journal of Philanthropy, author Amy Sherman writes that many churches provide the poor with food, clothing, and emergency financial aid, but with little personal attention to follow-up. Her criticism: the response of the church is no different than that of the government. She calls for the end of the "bigger is better" mentality saying, "It must go. Churches must not evaluate the effectiveness of their community outreach by the number of people they serve, but by their ministries' success in lifting families out of economic dependency. Too many churches are doing much and changing nothing; their outreach is a mile wide but only an inch deep. They are not helping poor people transform their lives; they are merely enabling the poor to cope a little better with their dysfunctional lives.... When churches successfully make the shift from throwing money at the poor to building relationships with the poor...tutoring children, teaching unemployed adults the skills they need to secure and retain employment...they begin to transform lives." What a challenge this presents to the church today. Are we up to it?

Who will lead us in the "new" vision of the church—which is not new, as it turns out, but is a solid, wonderful, Biblical model which desperately needs to be revived?

Any solutions must begin with restoring the father—or head of household—to his spiritual leadership responsibility, as set out in Ephesians, chapter five. Much loving, teaching, confessing, repenting, and discipling needs to take place for restoration to be realized. In the next chapter we look more insightfully at the crucial role of the father and how churches are unwittingly working against the spiritual leadership of the father.

Let us now turn our attention to the vision for building leaders who know how to lead a "household" of God.

One key purpose of the church is to build leaders. Leadership (spiritual maturity) is a central theme because God's desire is to see all of us mature in our relationship with Him. God wants to use each of us in the lives of others in order to bring about spiritual maturity. Building leaders is often undermined in a system of ministry that de-emphasizes or leaves out the role of integrated relationships in the maturity process. This chapter explains who leaders are and calls us to return to healthy spiritual relationships as the primary means for training leaders.

How The Church Can Build Mature Leaders

chapter 7

Who Is a Leader?

Depending upon your perspective, a leader can be defined in many different ways. Many churches believe strongly that men should be the ordained leaders. Beyond ordination, most churches do not seem to differentiate between men and women leading certain programs, such as Sunday school. I believe that what I am proposing in this book will work in any church. However, in an effort to defuse a potentially explosive situation with some readers, I will take a few minutes to clarify the position from which I write.

One of the fundamentals of God's design for family and church life is leadership. Leadership begins with God the Father. God instituted the role of family head, a role that is designed to be fulfilled by the father. I believe that any study of the scripture supports this fact. I cannot state strongly enough that any vision of reformation and revival, even such as I am proposing in this book, must include fathers and the church focusing on cultivating fathers in their leadership role.

However, we live in a day when many Christian and non-Christian homes are shattered by divorce and abandonment. This more often than not, thrusts the woman into the role of mother and father. This is indeed tragic, but I believe that a mother must look at how she can live out the role of head of household, as imperfect and difficult as it may be. I further believe that as the church moves toward a household approach to ministry, God's ideal is that these single moms be "adopted"by other families so that a father figure can model and help carry the load. I will go into how this can happen in more detail later.

As exemplified in the father, leadership is something that involves ultimate legal authority, responsibility, accountability, and is passed down through structures of authority. The father serves as a model for other leadership roles.

The heads of households are not the only leaders. Everybody is a leader to some degree. Older men, whether fathers or single, can be leaders. Older women, whether mothers or single, can be leaders. Young adults, even older children or siblings, can be leaders and should in fact look at themselves as such.

As a father, I want to be the primary leader of my wife and children. However, I am grateful for the leadership that older women in our church show my wife by teaching her wifely skills and answering her practical questions about how to be a good wife. Similarly, I want my older children, and other older children in the church, to lead my younger children through their example of love and service. Closely supervised and directed relationships between two children or two young adults can be life-giving and provide opportunities for growth when one is practicing mature leadership.

In summary, all of life's relationships, whether in the home, the church family, or in the unbelieving world should be birthed and guided by leadership, of which we are all partakers.

Where Does Leadership Begin?

Leadership basics are designed to begin in the home. God the Father leads fathers. Fathers lead mothers. Fathers and mothers lead their children. Older children lead younger children to some degree. Adherence to this pattern represents a complete multigenerational leadership chain. Obviously, broken homes have seriously severed this chain and the problems extenuate from there into our churches, neighborhoods, businesses, and government. I believe that if we restore the leadership chain in homes, we will, over time, begin to see restoration in all these areas.

Beginning in the home not only helps the home, it also helps the church, because as we have seen, the family is a microcosm of the church and has direct links to the church's viability. This is true because leaders of the home are by design the leaders in the church (I Timothy 3:4,5; Titus 2:1-8).

As you read this chapter please do not read passively, rather, read yourself into my statements. When I refer to the "father" and you are a single mother, unmarried, or a young adult, read yourself into what I am saying. We all should emulate many of the leadership characteristics of a father or a mother with those whom we lead. This does not put us in a position of usurpation. We are commanded to emulate Christ, but that does not make us Christ, does it? Care should be taken, however, not to cross over the bounds of authority that God has wisely set up.

When you see me refer to the family, also read "church relationships" into what I have written. When I mention a family spending time together, think about taking time to develop relationships within the church and so on.

Why Lead?

The leadership role is one of privilege and should be prized (even with all of its hardships). God tells us that it is good to aspire to positions of leadership (I Timothy 3:1) and, in fact, that those who lead will be rewarded both here (double honor) and in heaven.

Leadership means having an active role in the shaping and building of lives for future generations. Think about it. Each person is an original masterpiece that transcends time. God, the Chief Artist, has asked you to be His apprentice in shaping the life of one of His timeless masterpieces. **None of us are self-made masterpieces but the handiwork of God through our parents and brothers and sisters in Christ.**

Leaders impact family, church, and government. To do this, Christians need vision. As a parent, God desires to use you to shape the lives of your children, to implant in them a vision for what God can do through them. They will be tomorrow's electrical engineers, pilots, preachers, grocery-store managers, and most importantly, the leaders of tomorrow's families and churches.

Similarly, the church needs leaders to help raise spiritual offspring. Paul and the other apostles understood that healthy, maturing, growing adults were essential to the future of Christian families as well as to the Household of God. As discussed in the previous chapter, the parallels between raising children (physical and spiritual) are numerous. In raising spiritual children, we impact the course of personal, familial, national, and worldwide history because spiritual offspring can affect future generations for Christ.

Leadership reaps eternal rewards. Many rewards are to be enjoyed here in this life as we see our spiritual children grow into maturity. The apostle John often said how joyful he was to hear how the Christians were walking in the truth (2 John 1:4-3; John 1:3-4). We will have to wait for heaven to enjoy the best rewards. At that time, if not before, we will be glad that we eagerly shouldered the mantle of leadership.

How Are Leaders Made?

Now that you are convinced of your call to leadership, how do you get from where you are to where you need to be? Well, it just so happens that the relationship between a mature believer (leader) and one who is learning about the spiritual life is called "discipleship."

Bringing someone to maturity is not an easy or quick process. Maturity is something that is developed over a lifetime through all sorts of experiences. Life experiences provide the opportunity to apply biblical principles and respond with the mind of Christ.

Our lives go through many seasons. As children, we need to develop godly character, discern good friends from bad, choose a vocation, and seek a mate. As adults, we need to understand how to balance family life, work and a checkbook that always seems overdrawn. As grandparents, we need to understand how God's truths relate to the aging process and diminishment of physical and mental abilities.

When we properly apply doctrine to real life issues in a fallen world, we enjoy a far deeper relationship with God because we seek Him in all situations. Further, we have a unique opportunity to provide a witness to the unbeliever. These very practical issues are the same ones that unbelievers deal with, too. Therefore, if we are bringing all the issues of our life out, and examining them in the light of eternal truths, we are more likely to have something to say to a nonbeliever. For example, it is both helpful and hopeful for an unbeliever to hear how God has helped you overcome anger toward your spouse, or how God has helped you find fulfillment in your job. Talk about giving an answer for the hope that is within you! Many such testimonies, especially when seen first-hand, will also provide wisdom and understanding for our own children as they experience similar circumstances.

In short, being brought to maturity requires being connected through relationships which go deep into the real issues of life. Unfortunately, much of our current understanding of leadership training has not fully equipped us.

How the Current Ministry Model Conflicts with Training Leaders

The prevailing model of church ministry does much to split up relationships in the family and church. This division consequently does very little to train leaders beyond teaching doctrine in isolation, or other facts, which appear important but fall short of the goal.

Much injury has been done to ministry quality because of this change in understanding. Following are some examples.

The church is subtly seen as only one small compartment in our already overly busy, disheveled lives—not an organism of meaningful relationships (Acts 2:42-47; Col. 3:21). As a result, ministry is widely understood as something that is confined within the four walls of the building, not in homes, stores, ball fields, sidewalks, offices, etc. Through its focus on classes, it follows a model that focuses on the mind, not the heart, which requires relationship. Perhaps most tragic, leaders of the church are seen as professionally trained ministers, not fathers who have their households in order.

The average church works out its ministry goals in compartments. There is the evangelism compartment, the counseling compartment, worship, youth, education, home-schooling, and so on usually without coordination of schedules or objectives.

Thus, the church's identity as a unified force—a set of interconnected relationships—is lost in the shuffle. By allowing our churches to be exclusively need-driven or divided into groups by age and sex, we fail to equip people for the spiritual leadership of others.

Many programs are based on the old "school" idea of processing people through a curriculum until they can repeat back certain facts by rote. But someone in a profession, say a doctor, does not fully become a doctor by sitting in classes in school cramming their head with medical facts. They become a doctor by working with people. They become a good doctor by learning how to listen, empathize, and detect real problems beneath the presenting symptoms over time. A lot of time.

Even seminaries are alert to the fact that clergy need ongoing support and help with issues. This is why so many seminaries are providing ongoing mentoring relationships that go on long after someone has graduated and "taken a church." How is it possible to anticipate and answer all the questions and address all the life situations a person will encounter in a lifetime in the space of a few years in seminary classes? Of course it cannot be done, and this is why the face of seminary is changing.

We must honestly recognize the negative effects all of this compartmentalism is having upon our ability to prepare spiritual leaders. Mark 3:23 warns that a house divided against itself will fall.

One-on-one discipleship through relationships with those of greater maturity are what leaders need in order to be strengthened. Ministry that takes place "from house to house" or in the real life of the believer (Acts 2:42) makes this kind of discipleship possible. Why? When ministry takes place in home settings, where people are comfortable, it is easier to be more personal and more likely that meaningful heart-level communication will take place. These are important to the development of long-term relationships.

We need to adopt a long-term growth orientation which produces relationships that surpass programs in developing spiritual maturity and a willingness to accept the leadership of those God places over us.

Characteristics of Healthy Spiritual Relationships

Authority was, and still is, a key concept in God's plan. I am reminded of how the Pharisees constantly challenged Jesus' actions on the basis of authority (Matthew 21:23-27; Mark 11:27-33). Jesus was always operating within the constraints of authority. Clearly, God has established within relationships an order of accountability wherein our skills at handling life are to be lived out as examples to others (Ephesians 5:22-29).

The family unit has within itself an authority structure wherein the father is the head. Since this position is so primary, doesn't it make sense that we should be equipping fathers to be the spiritual leaders and "first examples" of maturity in their households? Can a weekly program do better than a spiritually mature man or woman right there on the spot?

Biblically, men are given the responsibility and authority to lead their wives and children. The pattern in scripture is for children to be with their parents in the meeting of the church (Exodus 10:9; Deuteronomy 12:6-7; Acts 2:46). The father is then to take what is taught and work with his children individually. His wife helps him fulfill this responsibility.

Beginning in Genesis, adults have had a problem accepting responsibility. We are prone to wiggle out of challenging or unpleasant situations. Accepting the responsibility to disciple others through one's own life is a daunting one. One that requires denying self and responding to the physical, spiritual, and emotional needs of others. It requires sacrifice of self-centered demands to extend oneself and grow for the benefit of others.

Romans 12:1 says that we are a living sacrifice. Of course, the problem with living sacrifices is that they are constantly scooting off the altar! Knowing human nature, we are all prone to take the path of least resistance, especially when it means denying self-gratification, or doing something that means work, challenge, and growth. A father who leads will often have to deal with his own sin before being able to help his family. Sometimes the memory of past shortcomings is a tool that Satan uses to lure us into defeat.

It is work to deal with issues at the heart level, and because we were never taught to lead it has become easier for many of us to allow the church to do our jobs. Those who aren't seminary graduates assume that leading is the job of the clergy. The tragedy is that when we release our responsibilities exclusively to the clergy through church programs, the heart is often left unaffected.

By pulling families apart, are we unintentionally overstepping our authority? Are we undermining an important "check" that God wants to use to spur family leadership to real spiritual growth?

Does One Size Fit All?

The further disadvantage of our current ministry approach is that we can slip into a mindset that dictates if a person does X, Y, Z, then they will be "equipped." Under this system, we will never be able to meet everyone's need for spiritual maturity. When viewed outside the framework of the household unit and its implications for leadership, vision, and accountability, the picture of a leader could be reduced to someone who has simply been given the title of an evangelism trainer, a counselor, or any number of jobs. This is horribly shortsighted, as we have seen.

That is why we must focus on discipling household leaders to meet the needs of the members of their households. But if we build healthy relationships, based on the understanding of a family, we will be in a better position to see individual needs met.

The division, weariness, and resulting failures spawned by the current "standardized system" has culminated in meager leadership fruit. God offers a better way.

How Is a Household-Based Ministry Approach the Solution?

I submit to you that in order to successfully train future leaders, we must change our method of ministry from our current age-segregated program approach to an age-integrated household approach. By a "household approach" I do not mean moving out of the church building, nor do I necessarily mean ceasing all age-specific activities or programs. It at least means that they need to go through a transformation. Later, we will address how churches can begin to change basic ministry structure so that they begin to follow this vision.

Core Characteristics

Following are a few core characteristics of a household approach. A household approach to ministry places an emphasis on building biblical households in which parents disciple their children and "adopt" other members of the congregation who do not have families, and where fathers practice spiritual leadership in the home. This approach builds a family-like quality in church life and ministry through emphasizing heart-level relationships, discipleship, and community. (I would like to thank Pastor Phil

Lancaster whose own thoughts are partially reflected in these characteristics.)

Restoration

The household approach respects and restores the father to his rightful place of leadership in the home. His equipping is both personal—through one-on-one discipleship by an elder—and corporate: he and his family are kept together as the rule, not the exception to the rule. He, in the context of his household, is equipped to lead his family. The household unit provides reciprocal accountability for the father and the individual members of his household.

Effectiveness

The spiritual gifts outlined in 1 Corinthians 12 are crucial factors in the maturity process and effective leadership. Gifts are often discovered through their use in everyday life! Within the household approach, fathers can discern and develop their gifts and the gifts of their wives and children.

The whole issue of spiritual gifts is one that does not fit too well into our current system because so much of what we do revolves around the use of the building on Sunday. The gifts of teaching and administration are obviously needed and used. They are built up before the body. However, other gifts are not seen as important. For the body to be healthy, we must help our future leaders develop their gifts and use them!

Ministry would be much more effective over the generations if fathers started to discern and develop their children's gifts and then channeled those gifts toward a life calling!

Imagine the Results!

Imagine how much more effective we would be if we

focused on equipping fathers as leaders:

1. Fathers would fulfill their leadership role in the home.
2. Children, especially boys, would grow up learning to be leaders. When they reach spiritual adulthood, they will be ready to marry and replicate the work for the next generation.
3. Selecting leaders (who hold office, such as deacons and elders) would be a natural and easy process because they will be known through the households in the church as a result of relationships.
4. Crisis counseling cases would dissipate because fathers are effectively discipling their wives and children.
5. Those disenfranchised individuals like singles and single-parent households will be "adopted" by older, more mature households so that they can be an integral, connected part of church life.

Now I want to take a look at the household discipleship vision which, when lived, results in trained leaders. We derive the vision from Deuteronomy 6: God's plan is accomplished over generations through heart-level relationships that are nurtured in everyday life. The four operative words here are generations, relationships, hearts, and everyday life. Consider this vision as the blood that flows through the veins of each member and ministry of the local church.

In the next three chapters, I will look at each crucial piece of this vision and draw applications for how it speaks to parents in training their children: our future leaders. This vision applies to more than just a father discipling his son! As you read, ask yourself if there is any element that does not apply to each member of the body of Christ.

A multi-generational theme is crucial to our effectiveness at building leaders. God has shown through many of the great people in the Bible how central generations are to His redemptive plan. By looking at some of the great families of the Bible, as we do in this chapter, we uncover some important lessons about the significance of a multi-generational approach to ministry. Our own role in redemption will be shaped by our view of God working through us to establish Godly generations.

God's Heart For Generations

chapter 8

God's method of discipleship is a beautiful process to observe in action. It is, simply put: applying God's powerful and living truths in close relationships. We must not fail to pass on the knowledge of God and a vision for His redemptive plan.

Consider God's instructions to His people, the very first time He spoke to us on these matters....

> Now this is the commandment, which the Lord your God has commanded me to teach you, that you might do them...so that you and your son and your grandson might fear the Lord your God, to keep all His statutes and His commandments, and that your days may be prolonged...And you shall love the Lord your God with all your heart and with all your soul and with all your might...And these words, which I am commanding you today, shall be on your heart...and you shall teach them diligently to your sons and shall talk of them when you sit in your house and when you walk by the way and when you rise up. (Deuteronomy 6:6-9)

God's plan is accomplished over generations through

heart-level relationships that are nurtured in everyday life. This is real discipleship and it needs to be rediscovered in the church today. While Deuteronomy 6 is a widely recognized passage, it is often under-used. It is a much richer passage than people give it credit for. Actually, about three-fourths of the passage is commonly overlooked. People normally focus on verses 7-9, which describe that parents are to teach their children as they rise up, lie down, and walk by the way. Forgotten are the other principles that when added to verses 7-9 make a complete model for discipleship.

From Deuteronomy 6 we learn that all parents "home educate". While some parents choose to home school, all parents, even all members of God's household "home educate"! By itself this maxim is a dramatic tool for building unity and leaders within God's household.

Many household leaders do not see themselves as educators of their children because the word "education" has been redefined by our culture to describe a purely academic, programmed process. This, coupled with the fact that for almost a century parents have been sending their children off to school every day has had a deleterious effect upon parents' understanding of themselves as home-educators or home-disciplers. As a result, fundamental needs like character, growth, morality, biblical virtue, and healthy relationship are not seen as part of the education process. **Education is no longer a process of learning how to learn, or learning how to be a spiritually mature person; instead, it has been reduced to the refinement of marketable skills, and the teaching of a worldview that is diametrically opposed to the Judeo-Christian view.**

Christian home "education" of any sort is a process that has as its goal the passing on of a God-honoring heritage from one generation to the next. Successful training of generations is training our children to train their children. This provides an understandable motive for our children to know why we are doing what we do. Whether we intend to or not, how we train our children does indeed set the stage for how they will train their children.

Let us examine the first part of God's plan to raise up household leaders. You and I have the chance to reach generations after us and to steer the course of our household for years to come.

From the beginning, God's plan has been to bring redemption to His people and creation at large. Man was created to glorify God and enjoy Him forever. The first picture of mankind that God gives us in His Word is one of being without sin and thus in harmony with God. Adam and his wife, Eve, were to serve God as described in Genesis 1:28b-30: "Be fruitful and multiply, and fill the earth, and subdue it; rule over every living thing that moves on the earth."

Of course we know the tragedy that followed in Adam and Eve's sin. Immediately, God injected hope...and the first outlines of His redemptive plan.

Genesis 3:15 says, "And I will put enmity between [the serpent] and the woman, and between your seed and her seed; He shall bruise you on the head and you shall bruise him on the heel." This is a promise that the evil deeds of the serpent will not ultimately triumph over God's plan. The triumph of God will come through the bearing of children (generations). One man (Jesus Christ) would come from the seed of the woman and destroy the works of the serpent—and we, His brothers and sisters, were to continue God's work after Him.

The spiritual training of children is an irreplaceable element in God's redemptive plan. Children are designed to carry on the redemptive legacy of their parents—passing on the knowledge and works of God to others. Thus, the household, God's unit for bringing redemption to man, was established first in Adam's household.

Today more than ever, households need the help of church relationships to pass God's redemptive plan on to their children. Perhaps there has never been an opportunity for the church to impact future generations as there is today.

By examining the work God did in, and through, the households He called, we can understand both the importance of God's plan for households and the works we can accomplish over generations.

Noah

In God's mercy, He selected Noah's household to be the unit through which He would sustain the human race and continue His redemptive work. Building the ark and filling it with two of every living creature was a household ministry. Noah's children played a central role in the process of redemption.

Through Noah and his household, God reminds us that He is holy and just and that our sin must be punished. The faithfulness and salvation exhibited through Noah's household pointed to the coming of a Savior who would take our sin and its punishment upon Himself so that we could be free to serve God.

Abraham

In Genesis 17:4 we read that Abraham was to be a father of many nations even though his wife was past childbearing years.

Years later, as if the wait for a son were not enough of a test, in a confounding twist, God called Abraham to sacrifice Isaac. God, however, provided a ram to take Isaac's place.

Through Abraham and Isaac, we are treated to a picture of our own redemption, which would be achieved through the sacrifice of God's only Son, Jesus Christ.

We also learn quite a bit about God's character and how we are used in His plan. We learn that God keeps His promises, no matter how impossible the circumstances may seem. We learn that God will accomplish His work in His time. But we must wait on God and not vainly try to manipulate Him when His timetable does not match our own. This points to the greatest lesson that we learn from Abraham and that is the centrality of faith in our relationship with God.

Joseph

Through Joseph's household, God saved His own people and the unbelieving Egyptians from famine. We see God's ability to work out His purposes despite man's sin. We see how important godly character is and how God can use His people to bring salvation and healing not just to His people, but to all peoples of the world. We further see a beautiful picture of reconciliation and restoration that takes place when we humbly admit our faults to one another.

Moses

Then there is Moses. Here's a man who, if it were not for his parent's faith, would have died before his first birthday. Imagine what the beleaguered Israelites would have thought knowing their future leader was hidden for three months and then sent floating down the Nile River.

We know, however, that God worked it out that Moses' mother would have the opportunity to raise him after all. When we give everything to God, He always rewards us.

God freed His people from slavery and fashioned them into a nation ruled by God's law. The pilgrimage from Egypt to the Promised Land was symbolic of our spiritual journey from slavery to sin to freedom in Christ.

Through Moses, we see the importance of leadership in God's plan. Moses was not a natural-born leader. God taught Moses the leadership skills he would need while he sojourned in Midian. He was not a man of eloquent speech, but God gave him the words to speak to Pharaoh. Moses did not know where to take God's people, but God provided a pillar of fire by night and cloud by day that would lead the nation.

As leaders of households we are called to lead. We do not have to be great orators or planners, we have to be humble and allow God to direct us in our leading of others to maturity. God uses our life experiences as tools to lead his little ones through the wilderness of everyday life to arrive at the promised land of maturity.

Joshua

Joshua was a courageous fellow. Being the son of a guy named Nun, he had to be. Given the faithfulness of Joshua at such an early age, we can infer that his parents raised him to fear and serve God. His faith extended into his own household leadership, as he is known for his statement, "As for me and my house we will serve the Lord." We should be as bold and specific as Joshua was in the leading of our own households.

Ruth

To the single women, single moms, or even widows reading this book, let the story of Ruth be an encouragement. Once again, it appears that God's team was down 49-0 and there were only five minutes left in the fourth quarter. Elimilech and his wife Naomi fled to Moab with their two sons to escape famine. Following the death of Elimilech and their two sons, Naomi elected to return to Bethlehem. Her daughter-in-law, Ruth, forsook her gods and chose to come with her. In His concern for generations, God provided a husband for Ruth named Boaz. Their marriage produced a son named Obed, the father of Jesse. Jesse was the father of David and generations later, the father of Jesus, the Messiah.

Not only does God care about the single mother, He does have a place in His plan for her and her household. As in the case of Ruth, He can provide restoration and healing. He can even provide a husband who fears God and with whom future generations may be raised.

David

We can learn quite a bit from the life of David. King of Israel, David was a man after God's own heart. Through his household, a temple where God could be worshiped was built. But his heart for God is contrasted by his sin of adultery and murder.

We should be encouraged by the example of David passing the vision of building God's temple on to his son Solomon. It is essential that we communicate the need to carry on God's work to our children. In addition, we would do well today to have a heart that seeks after God as David did. Like David, however, we are frail and sinful. Many today feel inadequate to lead because of past sin. David's example proves that there is always room for the repentant at God's table.

John the Baptist

The last words of the Old Testament (Malachi 4:6) are the same words that open the New Testament (Luke 1:17). "And he will restore the hearts of the fathers to their children, and the hearts of the children to their fathers..." After 400 years of silence, the promise was repeated to Zecharias that he and his barren wife, Elizabeth, would bear a son, whom they were to name John. The role of John the Baptist was to prepare the way for the Lord. Significant is how he was to prepare the way for the Lord. John was a forerunner of Christ who was to turn the hearts of fathers back to their children so that people would be ready for Christ.

Heart-level obedience to God's commands are vital signs of repentance. The people of Israel at the time of John the Baptist were in need of repentance. God's commands were necessarily tied to household life. "And these words which I am commanding you today, shall be on your heart; and you shall teach them diligently to your sons" (Deuteronomy 6:6-7). To return to household life, fathers had to have their hearts won back to their children.

Brothers and sisters, are the times in which we live that different from the times of John the Baptist? I would say not. What we are seeing God do today is what He promised He would do back in Malachi 4:6. Fathers are waking up; they're repenting of their failures in leading their households.

Generations in the New Testament Church

At the beginning of Acts, which describes the birth of the church, we see that the theme of generations is central. Peter's sermon at Pentecost begins and ends with a discussion about generations. Peter begins his sermon by quoting the prophet Joel (2:28-32): "And it shall be in the last days, God says, "That I will pour forth my Spirit upon all mankind; and your sons and daughters shall prophesy. And your young men shall see visions; and your old men shall dream dreams." The work of redemption is not simply an adult matter; it involves all members of the household.

Peter reiterates the original promise given to Abraham:

"'For the promise is for you and your children, and for all who are far off, as many as the Lord our God shall call to Himself.' And with many other words he solemnly testified and kept on exhorting them saying, 'Be saved from this perverse generation!' "Repentance was called for in the context of an appeal to future generations.

As a result, we see that three thousand souls were added to the kingdom that day. These were not just individuals but households: men, women, children, servants, and strangers. This event begins a recurrent theme of whole households coming to faith in Christ.

The life that was born from these repentant households provides a relational model of discipleship and ministry. "And they were continually devoting themselves to the apostles' teaching and to fellowship, the breaking of bread and to prayer.... And day by day continuing with one mind in the temple and breaking bread from house to house, they were taking their meals together with gladness and sincerity of heart" (Acts 2:42, 46). The work of God, beginning with repentance, was done in the hearts of households and pulled them together in church life.

We are in a unique position today to see whole household units come back together through repentance. If we focus more on reaching entire household units as opposed to individuals, we might be able to experience the incredible change that was so prominent in the early church.

Generations As a Tool

I would like to draw your attention to two instances which show generations to be a dynamic tool for the defense of the gospel. First, after healing the lame man outside the temple gate in Acts 3, Peter tells the unbelieving Jews that the healing was the work of God: "The God of Abraham, Isaac, and Jacob, the

God of our fathers has glorified His servant Jesus....And on the basis of faith in His name, it is the name of Jesus which has strengthened this man whom God raised from the dead...." By connecting Jesus to Abraham, a man whom the Jews respected, Peter sought to help them see that Jesus was indeed God's Son.

Second, In his defense before the Sanhedrin, Stephen drew upon the promise to Abraham (Acts 7:5) and referenced "father" or "fathers" eighteen times in fifty-two verses to emphasize the importance of generations as the center of God's redemptive plan.

How often today do we think this way? How useful is our lineage as a tool for the gospel? For many, the lineage starts with you. You must pass on the relationship to your children and their children's children so that they may be able to say that they worship and serve the God of their fathers! What an impact this would have upon those even today to hear from a person that theirs is the faith of their father.

As the gospel travels through the Jews and to the Gentiles we see God using generations through households in His kingdom's service.

Timothy

Of the New Testament heroes, Paul's disciple Timothy is a standout. When Paul wrote to Timothy, he made a special point of remembering his "...sincere faith, which first dwelt in your grandmother Lois, and your mother Eunice...." While Paul makes no mention of Timothy's father, we see the impact of a matriarch's faith of two preceding generations on Timothy. We see that the faith of a mother and grandmother plays a crucial role in the life and health of children. Further, we see how spiritual maturity is built by God, beginning with parents, grandparents, and then, as the child matures, other believers. It would appear that Lois and Eunice were the spiritual leaders of their households.

From this review, one can see how pervasive the theme of generations is in redemptive history. God has such a heart for generations. The evidence is overwhelming, and it will change how you think about your household as well as ministry.

A look at generations as we have just done uncovers some key interrelated truths that are vital to deepening our understanding of why generations are at the center of God's plan. In fact the following truths represent key elements that must be present. They are major aspects of the equipping process of future generations.

Children are Strategic

As we look back on this generational overview, more general truths emerge about God's leadership.

The first truth is that God loves children and sees them as of strategic importance to His plan. Consider that Sarah, Rebekah, Rachel, Hannah, Manoah (Samson's mother), and Elizabeth (John the Baptist's mother) were all barren women. God gave each of them children, emphasizing the importance of children in God's plan.

Further, one of the signs of God's blessing upon an obedient Israel was that "there shall be no male or female barren among you or among your cattle" (Deuteronomy 7:14). The law stipulated the death penalty upon anyone who kidnapped a child or adult. Jesus showed a love for children by taking the time to be with the children that people brought to Him, despite the protests of His disciples (Mark 10:14).

We find ourselves living in a society that does not value children. Abortion figures alone prove that point. But ironically in the church community, as pro-life as it may be, the importance of children is also diminished.

Do we see our children as leaders of future generations? As church and household leaders we need to understand the gravity of our responsibility. How well are our children and young people prepared to live their faith? Are they knowledgeable about basic doctrine and theology? Do they have well-developed convictions and vision for their marriages and households? Do they know what God specifically wants them to accomplish?

If we do not model a lifestyle of growth and purpose, who will?

Fathers Are the Leaders of Generations

The second general truth is that the role of the household leader is crucial. It is God's design that older, experienced fathers be the leaders of every generation. God works through those who are the keepers and purveyors of His covenant through generations. In Genesis 26:3-4 God renewed the promise with Isaac. He said, "I will establish the oath that I swore to your father..." We have no less need today for household and church leaders who, together, proactively lead with insight into the things that matter to God.

Men need to grow in responsibilities of spiritual leadership. A contrast between Abraham and Lot helps us to see how vital the father's leadership is.

Abraham was by no means perfect. But we see that his son, Isaac, went on to faithfully serve God. Lot lived with Abraham and stayed with him until the two had to split. We know what happened to Lot. Lot selfishly chose wealth and convenience but lost the hearts of his wife and daughters to carnality.

One of many lessons that can be learned from the contrast between Lot and Abraham is the importance of the father's leadership in fulfilling redemptive goals over generations. This is especially obvious in light of Abraham's faithfulness in the test of sacrificing Isaac. In contrast to Lot's daughters, Isaac was faithful to God's plan. In Isaac we see a trust in his father. Imagine being in Isaac's place on that altar and seeing your father raise the knife. Clearly the whole narrative in Genesis 22 indicates a submission and willingness on the part of Isaac to do what God had commanded. But notice how Abraham dealt with his son. He dealt with him on the basis of God's promises. Vision and purpose are central to Abraham's triumph in clearly the most demanding trial he ever experienced. Abraham knew God's promise—that he would make him a great nation through Isaac—and therefore knew that God would not take Isaac's life.

We never read of Lot seeking God's direction. Lot alone decided to pitch his tent toward Sodom. While Lot continued to get drawn into Sodom's wickedness, Abraham continued to experience great blessing, such as the birth of Isaac. Abraham knew God's promises and was walking in them.

The contrast between the failure of Lot and the success of Abraham presents a challenge for fathers today to be leaders who first of all understand the importance of the household unit in God's redemptive plan. Are fathers today motivated by a clear and convicting vision? How will future generations take greater steps for God's work if they are not handed a vision and promise?

This understanding should drive fathers to do as Abraham is described in Genesis 18:19: "For I have chosen him, in order that he may command his children and his household after him to keep the way of the Lord by doing righteousness and justice: in order that the Lord may bring upon Abraham what He has spoken about him." For a father to have this kind of relationship with his children they must "obey [God], keep His charge, His commandments, statutes and laws." This means basing their actions on the promises of God. Clearly, Lot showed no initiative to any of the above, and he and his household suffered for it.

God Works Despite Our Sin

One of the themes that is present in all of the households we have reviewed is that God uses imperfect people to carry out His plan. God forgives and heals sin in our relationships. Many who would be leaders never become such because they are weighed down by past or present sin.

An aspect of leadership involves redeeming areas of generational sin. When one holds the microscope to the lives of the fathers in the Bible, magnification need not be very strong to see that they were sinful people with sinful households. Murder, drunkenness, lying, kidnapping, incest. It is all there. General Hospital in the Old Testament.

Often, we see the sin of the parents—especially fathers—being repeated down through generations. For example, Abraham lied to Pharaoh about Sarah being his sister. Isaac, like his father, fell into the same temptation to lie to a foreign ruler, in this case Abimilech, about his relationship with his wife. Jacob, Isaac's son, was lied to by ten of his sons about Joseph's whereabouts. Some households have multi-generational struggles with drunkenness, drugs, illicit sex, and other sins.

Sin has multi-generational consequences that require the attention of the household unit to eradicate. In this sense, redemption is not just a personal process; it is a corporate process. Parents must humbly confess their own sins before God and their children so that their children might succeed where they failed.

God Deals with Generations

God is not surprised by our failures. He gives mercy to

those who repent and judgment to those who do not. It is therefore no surprise that His blessing and mercy extend to generations. "And His mercy is upon generation after generation toward those who fear Him" (Luke 1:50, Deuteronomy 7:9). God also judges generations. "For forty years I loathed that generation, and said they are a people who err in their heart, and they do not know My ways" (Psalms 95:10; Numbers 32:13).

God's focus on generations extends beyond the raising of faithful children (Christian household) to a group of people who are regarded as sharing some sort of common cultural attribute. Examples include "The Baby Boom Generation" and "Generation X."

We see God dealing with generations today. For example, the children of the sixties and seventies who rebelled against authority are now reaping what they have sown in that they are seeing their own authority over their children being stripped away.

Just as we saw in Joshua, God uses younger generations to bring mercy on older generations. One of the ways that God is bringing mercy upon the older generation today is through the younger households who home school. Through the home schooling structure, these households rediscover many forgotten biblical principles about relationships. God uses these households as instruments of His mercy on older generations when they share what they learn. By equipping our own children with a vision for producing faithful children, we are also equipping them to function as our Lord's ambassadors to unbelieving generations.

In summary, for generations to thrive, fathers must lead their households by living out and equipping them with God's redemptive vision. As part of this, fathers must be models of humility by confessing personal sin and helping the household as a unit to overcome multigenerational sin.

Our Redemption Is Multifaceted

The work of redemption involves more than presenting a cerebral outline of what one must do to be saved. The Fall extended way beyond man's mind. It has affected everything that was created. Sickness, death, and disorder were introduced. "Nature" is fallen. In Romans 8:21-22 Paul tells us that even the creation groans while awaiting its freedom that it was subject to through man's fall. Man's whole nature—his identity, his mind, his heart—is fallen. All of God's institutions—household, church, and government—are fallen. Work is fallen, in that it is laborious and in need of redemptive purpose. The immensity and pervasiveness of the Fall knows no bounds. The solutions of redemption go far beyond our personal salvation thrusting into all of life—medicine, education, science, politics, law and finance, the arts and literature.

Our goal should be to restore God's glory to every aspect of creation and the fallen world. Our sons and daughters must imbibe themselves in God's principles as we prepare them to live and work in a fallen world in order that they might be a willing instrument of God as He redeems it. The work of redemption is a mammoth challenge that requires a multi-generational vision.

Redemption Requires a Multi-Generational Vision

It will take generations to complete redemptive tasks. What one father starts may take three or more generations to complete. In this sense, Vladimir Lenin and Karl Marx, the founders of Communism, serve as albeit unfortunately, excellent role models. Their goal was to achieve the state of higher Communism, which essentially means worldwide Communism. Yet they knew that they would never achieve this in their generation. They were sure to trample all vestiges of freedom, which would prohibit the movement. Not surprisingly, one of the key components of their plan was to use the education system to indoctrinate the children in the core Communist values that would ensure its future development. Ninety years later, Communism still thrives (despite what the media says).

Redemption Reaches Unbelievers

Many great innovators and central figures in world history were Christians who sought to live out the mandate that was originally given by God to Adam and then passed on through generations. I am sure this statement sounds foreign to most peoples' thinking. The reason for this is that most of history, even specific church history, has been rewritten by those who hate God and Christianity. But we have allowed this to happen by withdrawing from positions of leadership in the institutions around us. We now find ourselves fighting on the world's terms, always playing catch-up ball, seldom setting the terms of debate. We need to take the offensive.

We need to develop and broaden a long-lost understanding of our place as Christians in society to reflect God's purposes. We are to use the talents God has given us to improve life for us and the world, while setting our focus on glorifying our heavenly Father.

In the life of Abraham, we see an explicit promise on the part of God to bless all other people, nations, governments, kings, and rulers through his descendants. "And in you all the households of the earth shall be blessed" (Genesis 12:3).

Woven through the fabric of history we see the recurrent theme that even those who do not claim to serve the God of the Bible have benefited from the application of biblical principles in their everyday lives, communities, and government.

If we want to truly bring the healing balm of the gospel to others, we cannot sit idly by and let our nation rot away into a humanistic, socialistic abyss. "Let your light shine before men in such a way that they may see your good works and glorify your Father who is in heaven" is the command of our Savior in Matthew 5:16.

If our gospel is ineffective in providing answers to our world's problems, if we do not see that God's principles in the Bible are the best ideas for solving America's problems, then we are most to be pitied and our faith is worthless. As Jesus said, "If the salt has become tasteless...it is good for nothing anymore, except to be thrown out and trampled under foot by men" (Matthew 5:13).

The Church Is Sitting on the Answers

Convinced that this world is lost to evil, much of the Christian church has withdrawn into a corner and narrow-mindedly focuses on "soul-winning". It has packed its bags and is simply holding on, waiting for the rapture. As the saying goes, "We have become so heavenly minded that we are no earthly good." We have turned Christianity into little more than a secret language confined to the self-imposed catacombs of our church buildings. We have thus abandoned all quarters of culture and society, leaving a vacuum of leadership to be filled by the impish enemies of our sovereign God. Try explaining to a child how it is that God, the Creator, who is sovereign, omniscient, omnipresent, and omnipotent, has nothing to do with life beyond salvation. What message does this send to future generations about how God governs all affairs of mankind? How are they encouraged and equipped to fulfill their part of God's redemptive plan, much less pass that vision on to future generations, with such a defeatist view? What vision of hope does this present to our children? Do not be surprised when those children live like the devil.

As parents we must be intoxicated with a desire to serve the Lord Jesus Christ through all that we put our hearts and mind to do. How can we glorify the Lord Jesus Christ through our service to our employers, our communities, our government? We have a right and a responsibility to share God's solutions to problems. This is God's redemptive plan. In this greater view, then, we can share the gospel, not just by word but by deed. People will see how what we believe affects what we do.

Redemption involves meditating on the big picture. Therefore, by focusing on the bigger plan, redeeming not just souls, but a whole fallen world in all its complexity, we can be the best witness. Our children must be equipped with this pervasive understanding of their responsibility. Their commitment must be strong enough to pass on to their children. It is through this system that God's redemptive work is to be accomplished.

We Must Think Long-Term

Having a multi-generational outlook means thinking long-term. Thinking long-term is difficult in a society that worships speed and efficiency. Many parents cannot wait until retirement to hop in the Winnebago and drive down to sunny Florida. Many of our nation's senior citizens have already done this, proudly displaying the bumpersticker, "I'm retired and spending my children's inheritance." In Deuteronomy 6:2, we read that God specifically tells parents that their responsibility extends to the third generation. God wants parents to see their responsibility as a long-term commitment that does not end when the children leave home or retirement.

Having a long-term perspective is crucial to raising children for at least two reasons. First, without it, many parents surely give up. Second, to produce faithful generations requires us to be oriented to the future, eagerly anticipating how our lives can contribute to God's work in the future. It will be difficult to expect our children to have a hopeful vision for the future if we are reluctant, passive and without hope ourselves. Short-term thinking is a perfect setup for failure. God continually reminds us to have our eyes on the future.

To help keep our thinking future-oriented, the Bible uses the following words: "remember," "testimony," "covenant," "generations," "inheritance," and "heritage". A long-term focus is crucial to persevere through the trials that we all encounter (Philippians 3:13-14; Romans 5:1-5). By thinking long-term, we can have hope. Our children can succeed where we have failed! But for this to happen, we must not let a bad day, a bad week, or even a bad year distract us and lead us into a detour of despondency.

One of the hallmarks of a great leader is his ability to offer hope to those who have no hope. Hope is an increasingly scarce commodity. But our God is a God of hope! As God's children and as leaders, we must share this sense of hope with generations. In the next chapter, I will take an in-depth look at heart-level relationships as vehicles for training leaders and communicating hope to those around us, and most importantly, to future generations.

Ministry is most powerful when it reaches the heart because it deals with the needs and struggles of the inner man. Heart-level relationships are crucial to building Godly generations and mature leaders. Relationship is what our Savior modeled in His ministry. The church would do well to rediscover this lost element. This chapter defines heart-level relationships and shows how vital they are to discipleship and ministry.

The Vision for Building Household Leaders

chapter 9

As our culture falls apart we feel great sadness. However, now is the church's greatest opportunity to reach a world of people feeling lost, alone, bruised, bitter, isolated, uncared-for, and in need of wisdom to live by.

This is the hour when the church can step in and equip its adults to be household leaders in both the traditional sense, and in the sense of including others as part of our "spiritual household." We may even have the vision...but are we up to the task?

Do we understand why spiritual growth and maturity require surrender to the direction of authority? If we, as supposedly mature adults, are still bucking leadership in our lives, what will we have to say to others about it? Or do we see submission to authority as a thing in the past—unnecessary, legalistic, or confining? Do we ourselves have a wounded or crooked view of authority? If we are deficient, how will we be able to accomplish God's plan of bringing His kingdom rule to this fallen world, and to our own disordered lives?

To renew our vision for the church we need to rediscover

the significance and power that exists in all aspects of human relationships. Through relationships the church can restore spiritual vision and a sense of goals. Not only do we need to value their importance; it is very obvious we need to rediscover how to have godly relationships. Deep, caring relationships are one of the sacrifices that our society, and the church, has made in its sprint toward self-gratification and self-fulfillment.

Godly relationships involving spiritual growth are not easy. All around us marriages, friendships, and households are falling apart because people don't want to do the hard work of building right and strong relationships.

Relationships Are God's Idea

God's redemptive plan unfolds through household relationships. Previous chapters have emphasized—albeit implicitly—the centrality of relationships in God's plan. If relationships were not central to God's plan, why did not He just lock the disciples in a classroom with a textbook? Certainly that would have been faster and easier. He could have made people with a computer brain, which could be conformed to the image of Christ with one or two upgrades. But God has ordained household relationships to be His primary structure through which the work of redemption is accomplished over generations.

God established a covenant with His children through the blood of Jesus Christ. A covenant is a formal relationship in which the involved parties agree to bind themselves to certain terms. God's covenant with His people is everlasting. He has saved us from our sins and we are to love and serve Him by seeking to govern our lives by principles found in His Word. When we as His children break that covenant relationship by sinning against Him, God does not leave us or forsake us. He remains faithful to forgive us when we confess our sin and repent. He accompanies His children through trials and tribulations that they might draw closer to Him and experience the joy and peace that can only be realized when our focus is on Him. This is the primary relationship that governs all others in our lives.

Fathers Model Relationship

As the head of the household, fathers are to model before their children the qualities of God the Father. The relationship that a father has with his heavenly Father sets the tone for relationships within the household. A father cannot give what he himself does not have. Fathers who humble themselves and learn the disciplines of surrendering their own hearts, minds, and souls will walk with God and experience deep, meaningful relationship with the master parent. Cherished qualities such as love, patience, forbearance, sacrifice, goodness, and gentleness will be his hallmarks, not because he has knowledge but because he has the experience of learning by living. It is this quality that transforms a dull brick wall into a stained-glass window through which God's love radiates beautiful light to all those around.

In this, fathers will be the priceless mediums through which their wives, children, and the church come to see the brilliance of the character and love of our God.

Marriage

The marriage relationship is a model of the relationship that Christ has with His church (Ephesians 5:22-29). In marriage we see restoration, sacrifice, intimate love, completion, protection, long-suffering, and mutual submission modeled. We see how two people can work together to accomplish part of God's broader plan of redemption. Submission is to be seen in the light of Ephesians 5:21—"Submit to one another out of reverence for Christ." In a marriage we should see not just a wife submitting to her husband, we should also see a husband submitting to the needs of his wife. This is what Christ did! We need to recapture the importance of submission in our relationships today.

Children

Children are part of the marriage covenant in that they carry with them the covenant promises given their parents by God to future generations.

Church leaders need to recognize that children and young adults need quite a bit of life guidance. They need relationships in which they can ask any question and get more than a doctrinal or theological answer that they could have found in a Bible encyclopedia. They need to be directed in how to think about God in a world that thinks little or poorly of Him. Only long-term, committed, safe relationships will provide this.

Total Commitment to Relationship

As the three relationships that I just talked about involve total commitment, so the ones that we develop in our churches need to have this same endearing quality. For it is only through the loving boundaries of a committed, long-term relationship that we will see people grow into spiritually mature adults.

I am reminded of a young woman who came to our church many years ago. She had been sexually, physically, mentally, and emotionally abused to such an extent that she had in fact spent many of her childhood years locked up in a closet. Her sullen appearance reflected the abuse, which had led to depression and her involvement in the occult. But this young woman was not sent away. She accepted the offer by one of the elders, Ron Boenau, to stay in his home. Over the course of ten years, this household (Mom, Dad, two young children) all but adopted her as their own. A relationship was born that would ride the stormy waves of suicide attempts, running away, and other dicey tests. That household never let go. The mother and father continued to love her, and teach her through their word and actions the freeing, healing truths of God's Word. This father and mother became her father and mother, and the two children became her brother and sister. Almost fifteen years later, this young woman is married and is managing a household of six children.

She still gets together with the household that took her in and nursed her back to health. Her "parents" still provide her counsel when needed. To me what is amazing is the total turnaround. A case like this would seem impossible to almost everyone. Any other way, a young girl like this would be just another faceless number in a sea of endless and mostly useless government programs. It was God working through a very endearing, long-term relationship that restored this young woman. If this does not put meaning to a new life in Christ then what will?

This relationship between this father and mother and the young woman they took in hearkens all the way back to the relationship Abraham had with God.

While the account of Abraham and the substitutional sacrifice of his son, Isaac, is one that is generally used to teach obedience, I think that an insightful treatment of the account goes deeper. Much deeper. This account was a test of two relationships: Abraham and God's; and Abraham and Isaac's. Obedience does not just happen in a vacuum. Heart-motivated obedience is something that grows out of relationships where a bond of trust, reverence, and respect exist between people. Consider that many struggles with disobedience in the home result from shallow relationships.

Abraham was a man whose relationship with God was so strong that he trusted Him in the face of a most difficult challenge. This of course was the command to sacrifice Isaac, his only son. This command seemed to contradict God's explicit promise to make Abraham a great nation through Isaac. How was Abraham able to calmly obey God in the face of such apparent contradiction? The answer lies in the relationship. Over time, he had come to know God and trust Him well enough that he knew that if Isaac died, He would at least raise him from the dead. He knew that God would somehow keep His promise to bring forth a nation through Isaac.

Are we as leaders as committed as Abraham was to God? Abraham put everything on the line which further deepened his trusting relationship with God. Like Abraham, do we today trust God to stay the course even when seemingly insurmountable problems face us? Going one step further, do we have the quality relationship with our children that Abraham had with Isaac? How would your child react to you if he/she were in Isaac's position and you were in Abraham's position? Clearly, the quality in the relationship between Abraham and God set the precedent for his relationship with Isaac.

The two relationships passed the test. God continues to fulfill His promise to bless all nations through Abraham's household. We must seek to be as committed as Abraham to God (our father) and our spouses and children.

Relationships are built on solid foundations of trust and character. God asks us to trust in His character, therefore our relationships must be based on trust. This trust should remain strong in the midst of life's messes, shown day in and day out over time. How else will people begin to understand the constancy and faithfulness of God?

Relationships Form the Basis for Discipline and Challenge

Discipline is not the bad word that it has a reputation for being. Discipline, correction, and reproof are key components of bringing someone to spiritual maturity. In Ephesians 6:1, just two verses after children are commanded to honor their father and mother, fathers are commanded, "do not provoke your children to anger; but bring them up in the discipline [nurture] and instruction in the Lord" (vv. 2, 4). Relationship is the framework wherein fathers are to discipline their children. It is also the framework for spiritual parents to help their spiritual offspring grow. If we are not practicing nurture and instruction in a loving and patient way, but instead are making threats or quick judgments without any basis in scripture, we will provoke our disciples to wrath.

The Heart in Relationships

If we are going to change course from the structuralism and the separation we now experience, we need to go to a level that is even deeper. For God's relationship to us flows out of His deep heart attitude toward us.

It is painfully clear that there are many Christian men, women, and children whose hearts are hard and cold toward God. The ironic thing is that often these are the same people we see every Sunday at church doing all we expect of them—attending youth group, going out on evangelistic visits, singing in the choir, or teaching Sunday school!

Hearts Must Be the Goal

I am reminded of a preacher who told this story—publicly—about his household. He had four children, all of whom are now married and serving the Lord. However, it was not always that way for one particular daughter. For fourteen years, she did all that was expected of her. She was as saintly as they come, setting evangelism records for her age at church. On the outside, she was a straight-laced Christian girl; however on the inside, her real person was someone antithetically different. When she was sixteen, she renounced her Christianity, left home, became involved with illegal drugs, and went through several immoral relationships.

In tracing his steps with his daughter, her father recalled a childhood instance wherein this daughter was caught lying about brushing her teeth. To enforce tooth brushing, her father instituted a system whereby each time they brushed their teeth, the children were to check off a box on a sheet of paper. His daughter checked it off for a fairly long period of time without ever brushing her teeth. The sibling "informers" were quick to bring this to their father's attention. Upon checking his daughter's toothbrush, which was bone dry, he confronted her only to find a defiant heart that eventually led to a clandestine rebellion. Initially, the parents tried to win the daughter by getting her to conform her actions to acceptability. This didn't work. They later realized that they were not dealing with her on a heart level. Then they changed course and began to rely on God to change her heart. It was God working His unconditional love through her parents that eventually changed her.

Cultivating a heart that loves God must be the goal. Our problem lies not in the goal so much as the method that we employ to try to reach that goal. It is easy to deceive another person when the other person does not know you well. The more you are around another person, the more opportunities you have to get to know them on a deeper level. You see them in different situations, how they act or react. The good points and the bad points have a way of making their way out. It is for these reasons that relationships are important. Without them, it is impossible to know people on a heart level. Today, many Christian parents do not know their children's hearts.

God Wants to Transform Our Hearts

God wants to transform our hearts into His image. Notice that the operative word here is hearts not minds. This is a summary of the message in the Bible. In Isaiah 29:13-14 God speaks clearly to the wayward Jews of the Southern Kingdom: "Because this people draw near with their words and honor me with their lip service, but they remove their hearts far from me." Psalm 119:9-11 gives us the reason why the heart is so important: "How can a young man keep his way pure? By keeping it according to Thy word. With all my heart I have sought Thee; Do not let me wander from Thy commandments. Thy word I have treasured in my heart, That I might not sin against Thee." God wants our hearts!

If all that God wanted was our minds, then the Pharisees would have been right. We could perfect ourselves simply by gaining knowledge and observing the law. Salvation by the mind is what the humanists believe. But we know clearly that there is such a thing as the heart. Each of us has a heart or spirit that is the seat of all that we think, say, and do. It is our hearts that are "desperately sick" (Jeremiah 17:9). There are over 200 different brands of psychology that try to help people deal with their mind and emotions. None of them come close to dealing with man's problems as the Bible does because it alone deals with the heart.

God Uses Parents to Get to Children's Hearts

God's primary plan for reaching the hearts of children is to work through the parents (Exodus 20:12; Ephesians 6:1-4). A child's heart that is turned to God is a powerful tool for faithful generations.

God sanctifies parents' hearts while working on the children's hearts. We must humble ourselves and first be teachable so that God can then use us to teach our children. Parents and other leaders can fall into pride. The humility of growth can give way to the pride of feeling mature. This breeds the misunderstanding that they are people with all the answers. They shy away from relating on a deep level because this reveals their weaknesses. However, it is in the sharing of our deepest secrets that people see that we care about and can identify with them.

Revealing our weaknesses often leads to dealing with sin. We need to heed the warning of Matthew 7:5. Before correcting someone else, even our children, we must first take the "beam" out of our own eye before taking the "splinter" out of their eye. This is one of the things that makes discipling future generations so difficult at times. The weaknesses we see in our children are often ones that we see in ourselves. We must humble ourselves and first be teachable so that God can then use us to teach our children. Heart-level relationships have a built-in check and balance system.

Success in Aiming for the Heart

God's definition of success is to walk with Him with clean hands and a pure heart (e.g. Psalms 24:4), trusting Him to provide our needs as we seek Him. Matthew 6:33 teaches that if we seek Him first, then He will provide for our needs. The scriptures are saturated with direct references to the heart and its centrality to a vibrant relationship with God. A long-lasting, developing relationship between parent and child is the road to the heart. This involves thinking differently, forsaking the world's systems, and clinging to God's precepts and promises. When the heart is right, everything else falls into place.

I am reminded of a conversation that I had with a father. For quite a while he and his wife were struggling with feelings of inadequacy because they were trying to follow the world's system of success in education...at home. They found that transplanting a humanistic approach to education at home didn't reap the spiritual reward they had set their sights on. What good was it for their children to get A's in math if their hearts were not knit with God? As if the weight of the world was off of his shoulders, he proclaimed, "God wants us to focus on the hearts of our children. That is what really matters anyway. We are doing the best we can and know that God will provide what they need in His perfect timing." How precious and insightful!

It is clear from the Bible that what is most important to God should be equally important to us. And high test scores, academic superiority, high salaries, multiple cars, and a nice house don't seem to be God's primary goals.

What Constitutes Reaching People's Heart?

Some would say that it is impossible to reach the heart—"only God can reach the heart." They are right in the sense that only God can know and judge a person's heart perfectly, and only He can change it. However, these truths do not obviate the fact that we can still perceive the condition of the heart and be one of God's tools for changing it in another person. Why would God put so many verses in His Word that deal with the heart if we cannot on some level know it?

Reaching the heart is a multidimensional pursuit. In the broadest sense, it involves being a model of what we believe. A model is something that you in some way want to emulate. The process that we take a person through is intended not just to help that person mature, but also serves as an example of how they should then disciple another person. A parent who reaches the heart must be self-giving. Like Christ, the giving of self includes everything—our time, our energy, our resources, our ears, our minds, and yes, even our own hearts.

In modeling, we set a standard and call the person to follow it. As parents, if we do not hold ourselves to the same standard, our example promotes hypocrisy. Self-examination is essential so that we do not look down on anyone and become self-righteous.

Taking Time to Communicate

In addition to our example, a vital dimension to reaching the heart is how we communicate. This begins with giving our time. God is so committed to relationship that He gave us the Holy Spirit to be with us all the time. What a statement! How do we measure up to this example? With more and more parents spending less and less time with their children, how can relationships be nurtured? How do parents model the Holy Spirit's example when they spend little time with their children? Opportunities to listen do not usually occur when it is convenient. By their nature, meaningful relationships are round-the-clock responsibilities. For a father, this may mean forgetting he's tired and staying up two extra hours talking to his son about whatever happens to be on his mind. For a mom it may mean stopping dinner preparations and taking several minutes to listen and converse with her five-year-old who rushed in from outside telling her about a cat fight she just saw. For a single adult, it may mean meeting with a fellow believer at five in the morning to talk with him about his job struggles.

While what is covered in such conversations may not seem important to the listener, it is to the speaker. Consider that teens who don't want to talk to their parents may have grown up in a home where the parents never wanted to listen. Ironically, in the early years when children never seem to run out of things to say, parents often respond with mindless "uh-hus". Then when those children reach the teen years, parents are ready to listen, but the teens have learned long ago not to talk!

Consider further that households are so fragmented throughout the week with each member pursuing their own interests that they spend very little time together talking. Household mealtimes, the most basic gathering time, are fast disappearing. Many households eat in shifts necessitated by out-of-control schedules. Parents often split up in order to cart their children to various activities. Household celebrations and traditions are not as important as they once were. Meaningful, substantive communication between children and their parents is disappearing. When households are together, they very often spend the time watching movies, which do little to foster meaningful interaction. Times together talking, eating, praying, reading, playing, celebrating, or working on a project, are times that build purpose, love, devotion, and structure into life. Very few of these things happen on a meaningful level today. No wonder the home is a solitary and boring place.

Consider the church. The church is fragmented, and long-lasting relationships are difficult to nurture. In many ways, the busyness of the home transfers into the church. The many demands of splintered interests in the home make it more difficult for the church. Although well-meaning, the church then exacerbates this busyness by adding more individualized activities.

We have become strangers in our own homes and churches. How well do we really—I mean really—know each other?

Listening is Elemental to Effective Communication

Attentive listening may do nothing more than plant another seed of trust with the person, but even if that's all that is accomplished, it is worth it. We have become so busy that our conversations have degenerated into putting out "brush fires," shouting orders, or telling people where we're going or what we want. Talking and listening builds trust which is essential to reaching the heart.

Good listening does not stop with the spoken word. It is not listening "to get to the point." Good listening involves asking questions that get to the bottom-line. Look for the motivation behind what is said or done. We have all been in situations where someone says something that does not agree with their facial expression or mood. Sometimes we accept what they say without further question. But at those times when we choose to probe beyond the surface, we often discover one, two, or even a whole proliferation of issues that are bottled up. These issues are the "heart" of discipleship, because these are where people truly are in life. This, not their outward expression, is where redemptive work needs to begin.

In cases like this when we stop what we are doing, sit down, and sincerely ask them to tell us what is going on, we seize a golden opportunity to build confidence with them and let them know that they are loved.

I am reminded of a young girl who angrily threw down a pair of jeans at her father's feet when she learned that she would be attending a private school where she would not be allowed to wear them. The dad, however, did not immediately reprimand his daughter but simply hugged her, told her that he loved her, understood her concerns, and then spent some time talking with her. As the conversation progressed, the daughter asked her father to forgive her outburst of anger (without his having to call her to repentance). Her initiative showed that her heart was repentant. As the girl looked back on it, she identified that experience as an important trust-building incident between her and her father. More importantly, she learned from the experience that her father accepted her, despite her shortcomings.

I suppose her father could have immediately rebuked her

for her anger or marched her down the hall to be disciplined. But his approach produced fruit that surpassed repentance. He took the opportunity not to push her into outward conformity, but to show that he understood how she felt. He knew from his own personal experiences that going to a new school and making adjustments was tough.

There is a lesson in this for parents and all adults who are responsible for children. If all we want to do is produce people who look like Christians, our responsibility is fulfilled when people say and do the "right" things. Mass-producing perfect "Pauliannas" misses God's purpose and misses the opportunities to develop heart-level relationships.

A pastor I know recently gave a presentation on "Getting to the Heart" at our church. As part of his talk he gave us the following questions that he termed "X-Ray Questions for the Heart."* These are questions that he uses to cut through the small talk and the righteous veneer to get to people's hearts. Some apply more broadly than others. Anyway, they give an example of what heart-level communication is.

1. What do you love? What do you hate?
2. What do you want, desire, wish for?
3. What are your goals and hopes? What do you pursue?
4. What are your plans and intentions designed to accomplish?
5. What do you fear? What do you NOT want to happen? What do you worry about?
6. What do you think you need?
7. What really matters to you?
8. Where do you find comfort, escape, pleasure, security?
9. Who do you trust? On what or whom do you set your hopes?

10. Who must you please? Whose opinion counts?
    From whom do you desire approval and fear rejections?
11. Who are your heroes? What kind of person do you want to be?
12. How do you define success or failure?
13. What makes you happy, rich, secure?
14. What would give you the greatest pleasure?
    The greatest pain?
15. What do you see as your rights?
16. What do you think about, talk about, pray for?
17. How do you spend your time? What are your priorities?
18. What are your beliefs about life, God, yourself, others?

Is such a vision too good to be true? Absolutely not! A vision where the church, God's household, lives in enduring heart-level relationships that teach, encourage, and challenge as a fulfillment of God's plan is within our grasp. In the next chapter, I will reveal the simple but crucial element of relationships that allows us to get to the heart.

* From a talk by John Thompson, teaching elder at Grace Bible Fellowship, Walpole, New Hampshire.

How do we unite generations in ministry? Through heart-level relationships that are nurtured in everyday life we can model a life that reflects the powerful truths of God's word. More importantly, when real life is the context for teaching these truths, we give others a true picture of who God is and how He can help them overcome struggles and challenges. This chapter will look at specific ideas and examples for bringing truth to everyday life!

Bringing The Truth To Life

chapter 10

Referring to Christians, the illustrious professor of Christian Education at Dallas Theological Seminary, Howard Hendricks, once said, "The problem is not that we don't know enough, but that we don't live what we know."

Many of you have no doubt done battle with the kitchen drawer where you keep your leftover containers. Each bowl and lid is a different size and shape. After frantically groping through the drawer to find matching bowls and lids, the remaining bowls and lids are so disheveled that one finds it difficult to shut the drawer. What a mess!

This serves as a pretty good analogy to describe the Christian life. There are many important principles and beliefs, but they are hard to remember and put to good use. Our churches shovel out tons of information. We assume that because we are teaching, the people are learning. But coverage does not ensure life application. The result? A chasm develops between what we say and what we do. The practice of Christianity is therefore blown off in the world's eyes as hypocrisy, bigotry, and intolerance.

Deuteronomy 6:7-9 calls us to practice our faith as a lifestyle to be lived out before our children, our communities, and our government. It is within the milieu of everyday life that we will be able to reach the hearts of future leaders. In order to be a lifestyle, our method for teaching must be in harmony with the message, or else the message itself will be distorted. In his widely read book Christian Education, Lawrence Richards writes,

> The classroom setting has dangerous implications for Bible teaching. In our culture, classroom treatment of any subject matter tends to clue learners to process that content as academic. And the academic is perceived as "unreal" in so far as present experiences, feelings, attitudes, and values are concerned. This is particularly tragic for Christian education. We communicate a revealed truth that must be perceived as life and integrated into life. If our method of communication is not in harmony with the message communicated, we distort the message itself. (p. 191)

Spiritual training must go outside of these confining structures and encompass all of life as it is experienced through everyday activities. How else is it possible to bring God's principles to bear on all of life?

Judge Robert Bork in his book, *Slouching Towards Gomorrah* has a whole chapter dedicated to the connection between the decay of our culture and the ineffectiveness of religion. Quoting Albert Lewis in 1920, he states that "religion is declining because those who identify with it don't actually believe in it" (p. 280). The essence here is that there are a lot of people who claim to believe many things but do not apply what they believe to how they live.

As a church, we need to be growing leaders who understand how to live, and will pass on in everyday life the truths about who God is and His vision for us. God in His great wisdom has made this His plan for teaching others, and there is a dual benefit. Often when we teach, we will come away learning more than those whom we are teaching. This is true because teaching someone has the effect of cementing what is taught in the mind of the teacher. This makes teaching and learning a redemptive process for both pastor and church member, adult and child.

The Crucial Difference

Let's take a look at some principles of lifestyle teaching.

How can a parent demonstrate that the Word extends to all of life? Imagine a father who decides to teach his son how to fish by placing fish in the bathtub for his son to catch. The bathtub setting does not provide the elements that must be taken into consideration if one is going to catch fish in a lake, stream, or ocean.

Fish are not simply caught. A successful fisherman must take into consideration the elements of water temperature, water color, wind, underwater structure, time of day, other fisherman, and so on if he is going to catch fish!

So while the son may catch a fish in the bathtub and the father may declare him a successful fisherman, he is no more equipped to catch fish than he is to build a skyscraper. Why? Because the context where the fishing will take place has direct bearing on the method used to fish.

It is the same way with teaching biblical principles.

If we limit our teaching to the classroom or even the family room, our children will indeed come away with a dif-

ferent understanding of the Christian life. Why? Because the meaning of the message is conveyed in the way it is taught. What is taught outside of everyday life will be hard to apply to everyday life.

There are two avenues for teaching in everyday life.

First is the use of concrete objects to teach a biblical truth. Jesus used ordinary objects to teach truth. Why should we depart from His example? This approach works especially well with children but can also be helpful with adults. Second is the use of events—even seemingly insignificant events—that happen during the course of the day to show how truth is applied. In either case, even the most cerebral principles can be brought to life in living color.

The use of objects to bring truth to life

Let us take a look at a few examples of how objects can be used to bring truth to life. Oil filters are a greasy fact of life for most of us, but changing the oil filter represents an opportunity to "lifestyle" teach!

An oil filter cleans the oil that passes through the engine of your car. Oil filters can remind us of 2 Corinthians 10:5, which in principle states that God's Word is to serve as a filter for our thoughts. In addition to a disciple learning this simple truth, he is developing a deeper relationship with the discipler by virtue of the fact that they are spending time doing something valuable together. The disciple learns a practical skill, while at the same time learning that his relationship with God extends to activities as simple as working on the car. With reinforcement through a consistent diet of similar experiences, such teaching will provide a spiritual heritage for the disciple. Attaching a biblical principle to an everyday activity helps to ensure that the principle is remembered and passed on for generations.

For the discipler, this is an opportunity to add to the reservoir of time that will strengthen their relationship and open free-flowing communication. The more opportunities he has to be with his disciple in a variety of settings, the more opportunities he will have to observe the heart. This affords him the opportunity to nip character flaws in the bud that later may develop into spiritual land mines if left alone.

Think of a mother who has her child help her prepare a meal in the kitchen. In the process of measuring out ingredients, she remembers to teach her child that just as the measuring cup assures the proper amount of ingredients that are used in the recipe, the Ten Commandments are one of several biblical "measuring sticks" to determine if we are living in accord with God's word.

The mother can also include practical applications from her child's math studies. In this scenario, math is necessary in order to double or split a recipe. The biblical principle of order can also be taught. God is a God of order. Everything that we do should be done in an orderly way. We can be reminded of this when we follow directions in a recipe.

Using concrete objects helps younger and middle-school children because they are concrete thinkers and do not have a handle on the abstract. While these two examples include parents relating to their children, the principle applies to all discipling relationships. Adults, too, can benefit from the experience of tying spiritual truth to everyday objects.

The following example is much broader and includes how the everyday-life approach is a powerful evangelistic tool. I will admit at the outset that this example is a bit exaggerated, but it gives some ideas of what might be said in an everyday life situation.

A father (we'll call him Fred) wakes up Saturday morning. Topping his "Honey Do!" list is washing the family van. He knows that involving his son will take more time, enough time that he could possibly miss the football game on TV. He determines, however, that missing the game is a small price to pay for the long-term benefits of taking another opportunity to deepen his relationship with his son, Johnny.

Fred takes a few minutes to stop and plan what he is going to teach his son while washing the van. Upon going outside and getting the hose hooked up, his son's friend Mike comes over and asks if Johnny can play. Johnny tells Mike that he is about to help his father wash the van and proceeds to invite him to help. Mike accepts.

Mike has an older sister and lives with his mother, who has been divorced from her husband, Frank, for two years. They are new to the neighborhood, and Fred suspects that they are not Christians, so he takes this as a golden evangelistic opportunity.

Fred starts by reminding Johnny that washing the van is a form of stewardship. Fred explains that God in His sovereignty has provided the van and that it is their responsibility to take good care of it. Washing it is therefore as real a form of stewardship as is their tithe.

As the boys spray the van and wipe the dirt off with the sponge, Fred begins to share the gospel using the activity as an analogy.

Addressing Mike, Fred asks, "Did you know that your heart is as dirty, even dirtier, than this van?" Mike responds, "What do you mean?" Fred proceeds to explain the gospel message to Mike—that Jesus has died to take away our sins so that we can serve God and have joy and peace.

After sharing the gospel, Fred asks Mike if he would like to pray to receive Christ. Mike says, "yes!"

After finishing the van, Fred takes the boys inside and sits down to pay them for their help. Instead of giving each of the boys a crisp one-dollar bill, he chooses instead to give them each ten dimes. He explains another principle of stewardship, the tithe, and ties it into Johnny's math lesson on decimals. What can seem stoic and irrelevant in a textbook gains relevancy and meaning when it is applied in real life. Fred asks, "If the tithe is ten percent of what we make, how much should each of you boys set aside to give on Sunday?" The boys think about it, move their dimes around, and come up with one dime apiece.

"Great!" says Fred, who then goes on to help them understand that the primary principle in math is order. "Decimals help us to see order in numbers. When we study and use math, it should remind us that our God is a God of order and that we should do all things in order."

The Use Of Events To Bring Truth To Life

Every day, we walk through many different experiences. Some happy, some sad, others inducing anger or despondency. In some, we succeed in faithfulness to God. In others, we fail. These little interludes, good or bad, make up pages in our book of spiritual inheritance to be passed on. Like books, they are intended to be read by others so that they may glean life-giving comfort, teaching, and direction. Most people do not see their experiences as being all that meaningful to themselves or to others, so they withhold what they have learned. If the life-giving pages are never shared with others, they will yellow and eventually crumble in rot.

I have a friend who is slowly going blind. I meet with him regularly and he reports on the worsening condition of his eyes. He never is despondent. He always says, "God is good" and continues to show incredible peace and acceptance of God's providence without any anger or self-pity. His words and life are a constant reminder of God's goodness.

One of the most memorable prayers I ever heard was a blessing that thanked God for taste buds. Ten years later, I am often reminded while eating how good God is to give us taste buds so that we can enjoy all sorts of culinary delights. It is a further reminder of the great wisdom and creativity of our God. I have drawn closer to God because of that prayer and have yet to meet someone whose awe of God is not increased because of the wonder of taste buds!

Going to the grocery store or paying the bills is a regular reminder that God provides for our needs. A leader who has just survived a major car accident has a great tool for teaching about the sovereignty and care of God. A leader who teaches his disciple the importance of the tithe by tithing himself, even when he admits he "can't afford to," teaches by example when he always seems to have enough money anyway.

Experience, especially bad experience, is a good teacher. In some cases it takes a great amount of humility to tell someone about something that we did which was wrong. I think that it is in these humbling situations that God can use us the most. When we admit to failure it is like a huge wall comes down allowing others to see us as someone who can identify with their weaknesses. Jesus identifies with our weaknesses in order that we may call upon His strength!

Not too long ago, a friend was staying at my house, and he related how he had made some selfish, ill-advised investment decisions about seven years ago. He told me how as a result he reaped strife with his wife and his cash flow. But he also told me how God had provided a flexible, part-time sales job that would allow him to pay off the debt he incurred from the bad investments. Even in dealing with sin's effects, God often extends His loving and merciful arms to us when we deserve to reap bitter results.

Think of a man who comes home from work and says to his children, "I was furious at my boss today, and rather than going and talking out our differences, I had a bad day and really didn't get much work done. I was wrong to be angry and not work out the problem. I'm glad God showed me that, because I don't want to live with a bitter heart. I will go to my boss tomorrow and ask his forgiveness." This is relational, biblical-principle-based teaching, from a parent to a child, in life.

Think of the parent who gets caught speeding attempting to get her son to hockey practice on time. But instead of driving off muttering about getting caught while everyone else speeds along, she decides to talk about it with her son. She uses the opportunity to tell her son that she was wrong for what she did and that God wants us to obey those in authority.

About fifteen years ago, a married man in our church got angry with his wife and shot her in the head. Miraculously, the wife survived. Her husband went to jail. Years later, however, the man repented of his sin and asked his wife's forgiveness. Today they are still married. I know this man fairly well. I remember his telling the congregation about what he had done and how he had given God the glory for reuniting he and his wife. This was the most powerful example of God bringing healing and forgiveness I had ever seen. To this day, it serves as a reminder of how great God's power is, even in the darkest circumstances.

I Get It!

Someone has said, "Truths are caught, not taught." In fact, we need to hear spiritual principles which affect our lives more when we see them enacted in life situations like our own. What you saw in the above examples was the coming together of relationships, biblical principles, academic studies, evangelism, and normal everyday activities: in other words, the truth in life. **When we use everyday activities and events to teach others about God, we develop a lifestyle that helps us grow as Christians and demonstrates our faith to others.** Truth in life is truth that will be passed on through future generations.

Remember that Jesus used the common events of life to teach theological truths. His method was to build upon what was already known to those whom He was teaching. He used mustard seeds, trees, rocks, money, wine, and children as the springboards for teaching truth. He spoke and acted with grace when people were caught in sin and foolishness. It is the duty of all leaders to be open to God's truths first so that they can present them to others in life's great and small activities.

With a little thought, the opportunities afforded by everyday life are limitless. The only thing that you really need is to take the time to think and plan ahead to bring all of these facets together. This is difficult to do in our day, but it is something we must do. In time, it does get easier as we train ourselves to think that way. We learn to watch for opportunities, temptations, spiritual dry spots, anger, and sin in our own life, and in the lives of others. These are our open doors to "speak into" the life of another.

If we lose the ability to reach from life, to teach in life, we have lost crucial ground. Everyday life is where we ask our most honest, basic, and important questions. It is where we are most open to answers.

Many Christian leaders are wondering how the church will fare in the coming century as western culture slides deeper into postmodernist thinking and a "tolerant" approach to sin. How will we prepare those who are coming up after us to season the world with the true knowledge of God? Parents are concerned too, having seen the children of other Christians grow up and leave the faith. How will our children fare when they have to negotiate the curves and sharp turns of life out on their own? Will they live as believers, much less pass on their faith to others? Or will some unexpected event bump them off-road altogether?

We need lifestyle teaching and churches that will incorporate a church-and-home mentality into their vision if our churches are to walk with God and pass along their faith to a spiritually dark generation.

In the next chapter we will look at Christ and his gospel as the essential foundation upon which to build ministry that focuses on heart-level relationships that are built in everyday life.

Stages in Rebuilding

Part Four

For the vision and plan presented in this book to have an impact, we must rebuild upon the gospel of Jesus Christ. We must avoid the legalism that has enmeshed many churches in guilt-induced, performance-based spirituality. We must be messengers of God's grace into the lives of others. This chapter explains who we are in Christ and how His relationship with us is the foundation for our relationships with others.

Rebuilding On Christ And his Gospel

c h a p t e r 11

Take a look at any industry leader and you will see that they know the value of constantly reevaluating their product and processes. They would tell you that "standing still is moving backward." New technologies and trends make it possible to make a good product or service even better. Corporations downsize, streamline, and reorganize all the time. What about the church? Do we reevaluate our goals? Do we rethink our methods and programs in light of God's Word? What are our spiritual growth goals? We would do well to go back to the Word and reevaluate our goals and methods.

Let us begin with goals. Many church leaders today have growth as a goal. But what is meant by growth? Is it numerical or spiritual? There is a whole industry to help churches attain the former but with comparatively little success in the latter. I believe that if we are effective at growing spiritual leaders, we will see numerical growth. But seeking numbers does not usually lead to heart-level, life-changing, spiritual growth.

If the primary goal is heart-level, life-changing, spiritual growth then the sixty-four-thousand-dollar question is how can our churches achieve it in our members? What methods should we employ? It would be easy at this point to begin thinking mechanically and evaluate programmed activities for their effectiveness at building maturity.

While programs can be a useful tool, by themselves they are woefully inadequate. They are only our best efforts to organize teaching and people. They are not sacred. But God's relationship with His people is sacred. We need to reevaluate how we are helping people come to know Him and making their lives accessible to Him. We need to dig deeper to find the true source of life-giving water.

Spiritual growth is the result of the Holy Spirit applying the work of Christ in our lives. Jesus Christ is the "author and perfecter of our faith," He is the "cornerstone," the "beginning and the end." In other words, it is He, not our ministries, programs, or activities that causes real, heart-level, life-changing growth. He gives us the life-giving water of growth through our relationship with Him. As we walk with Him and get to know Him, we more deeply understand how great His provision is.

Ministry on all levels flows out of our relationship with God. Christ's direction and strength for ministry emanated from His relationship with His heavenly Father. What was true for Christ is also true for us. Our relationship with God is the womb through which our relationship with others is born. If our relationship with God is mediocre, we cannot expect to be all that effective with other discipling relationships. However, we have gotten away from this understanding. Instead of seeking spiritual growth, we are often fixated on numerical growth. Instead of letting the Holy Spirit work through us in His timing, we impatiently try to conjure up growth by seeking numbers.

How then do we get back to focusing, relying and trusting

in Christ for the power and results in ministry? How does He affect our methods?

How Who We Are in Christ Affects What We Do and Why We Do It

Our own identity is rudimentary to ministry because how we understand who God is and what He's done for us affects how we work with other people. If we are trying to help people become more like Christ, we had better know who He is and how He relates to us. Unfortunately, I think we have come a long way in the wrong direction and lost that beautiful picture of who He is. We need to once again grasp the depth of how great our salvation really is and the enormous provisions that are ours through Him.

We are God's sons and daughters, eternally adopted to share in His inheritance with Christ. Orphans live in fear; they fight and connive to survive because they are not secure. But as His children we are already totally acceptable to God and cannot improve our standing with Him through our works. It is wrong, therefore, to look at life as a struggle to earn our Father's favor. Our acceptability is based solely on the work of Christ, not our own works, no matter how great we may think they are! We are free to walk with God because He will never leave us or forsake us because He cannot reject His own. We can therefore serve Him out of love, in gratitude for what He has done and continues to do to enrich our lives.

However, it is often the case that we associate our acceptability to God with how involved we are in the church's ministries. We figure, if we are doing more, then we are more pleasing to God. Nothing could be further from the truth. This essentially is a works-righteousness mindset. Such a performance standard will mitigate against an appealing relationship with God.

How does this attitude represent Christ? How does it help those tired, hurting individuals who are desperately looking for acceptance, security, and solace from the cruelties of life in the twenty-first century? How do we help people who are tired of performance-oriented living?

In Luke 10:38-42 we see that Martha struggled with this. After inviting Jesus over for a meal, Martha allowed herself to be distracted with cleaning house and meal preparation while her sister, Mary, simply sat at Jesus' feet drinking in every word He uttered. Jesus lovingly and gently rebuked Martha for her misplaced priorities.

The plans and dreams of the Lord's servants can easily become an end in itself, rather than a means to the end of serving Christ. We tend to get so focused on making ministry work that along the way our focus shifts from Christ and being faithful to Him to a focus on our own works, and their sufficiency to please our Lord. Like a flash flood sweeps a car off the road, busyness in ministry can easily take our focus off of Christ. To be faithful to God we must trust Him to work in and through us and use our lives to relate the acceptance, security, peace, rest, and love to be found in a personal relationship with Christ. These (and many more) are the benefits of our adoption and should drive how we minister. If they do not, we misrepresent Christ, the source of life to others.

Trusting in Christ to Do What He Says He Will Do Through Faith

In Matthew 14:22-36 we read the familiar account of Peter walking on the water to meet Jesus. Allowing the wind and waves to shake his faith, he began to sink.

Relationship ministry will test and challenge your faith.

There will be times that you doubt whether there is any growth taking place, in yourself and others. There will be times that you are tempted to cower away from developing relationships with others because of fear of rejection. Opening up to others can be a little fearful. But we learn from Jesus that we are made strong in our weaknesses. We need to acknowledge our weaknesses because it is through them that the power of Christ can best be seen. Unless something prods us, we will always stay in our comfort zone and end up achieving very little in the lives of others.

Further, we cannot fabricate what only faith can do. Only God, not our ministries, can change the hearts of people. Only God can take an unloving husband and make him loving. Only God can change the heart of a teen who is in rebellion. Only God can change the heart of a young man who is living with his girlfriend. Only God can build a group of households into a unified church. In each of these and other circumstances, we must have faith in God, not our best efforts, to bring about the outcome.

We read in 1 Corinthians 3:6 that we can plant and water, but it is God who brings the increase. We must rest in the promise that God will do what He says He will do.

Faith involves waiting on God. This involves continuing to bear with our fellow believers in love and prayer, especially through times of spiritual drought. It involves hanging on to the promises of God like that in Hebrews 13:5, where He promises not to leave us, nor forsake us. Further, in Philippians 1:6 we see that God will complete the work he started in each of us! The problem is, we live in a day when instant gratification abounds. To wait is to die a slow death. Our heavenly Father takes His time to work out His plans for our lives. We simply must rest in the understanding that ministry and spiritual growth is a process, not an event.

Faith is easier when we think in terms of relationships.

Again, let us think back to God. God does not just dump on us all at one time all that we are doing wrong. Nor does He bring us into perfect conformity with His will all at once. Both of these aspects of our relationship with Him are dealt with through our relationship with God over time. Should we be any different in our ministry with others?

God does not rant, rave, and threaten us when we struggle or sin. God lovingly and patiently convicts us and promises never to leaves us. It is vital that we model the same love, patience, and security with our brothers and sisters in Christ and our friends if we want to have an impact upon their lives. We need relationships of faith so that we will not fall into lifeless programs as we teach people how to have a personal walk with the Lord.

Faith Working Through Love

Rebuilding on Christ and His gospel means grace working itself out through love. Jesus rested in His Father's love and goodness. He trusted Him, not seeking his own will but that of His Father. He said that the second-greatest commandment is to love your neighbor as yourself. Paul tells us in 1 Corinthians 13 that the greatest gift is love. Love, the hallmark of our Savior, needs to be reapplied as a basis for our ministry efforts.

Our ability to love others as Christ does emanates from our own relationship with Him. In Luke 7:36-50, we read that Jesus told Simon the Pharisee that "he who has been forgiven much, loves much." Those who are ensconced in a whole list of man-made rules and legalism really do not understand the depth of their sin and the glorious remedy in Christ. Rule-keeping leaves little room for loving those who don't agree with the rules or follow them poorly. To counter this, we must preach the gospel to ourselves everyday. Paul, at one time a Pharisee, understood that the tendency is for Christians to resort to rule-keeping and performance standards.

In Romans 7:7-25, we see that Paul is preaching the gospel to himself and proclaiming the power of God for forgiveness. **The gospel is not just an outline that we give to a nonbeliever; it is the lifeline that connects us to the source of power for daily living and loving.** The truth that "there is now no condemnation for those in Christ Jesus" needs to be at the forefront of our daily life.

As we preach the gospel to ourselves every day and experience God's forgiveness, we live in Christ's sufficiency, not our own. Our sin is no surprise to God, and because we are already totally acceptable to Him, we can run to Him not having to fear His reprisal or displeasure. We do not need to try to earn back His favor, because we already have it through Christ's work.

As we are constantly gripped by this truth, we are freed from the guilt and shame of our sin. We are able to love others. "He who is forgiven much, loves much." Living a life of repentance, preaching the gospel to ourselves every day, and living in the sufficiency of Christ is the way to live fully and joyfully. This fans the flame of spiritual maturity and faith working itself out through love. This also is the picture that we want others to have of what it means to be a Christian.

A household approach to ministry communicates love because it is based on relationships not attending certain programs or even conforming to certain rules (as well-intentioned as they may be). Jesus gave no entry requirements. He accepts us not on the basis of how we act but on the basis of what He has already done for us. Remember that it was the Pharisees who based their "ministry" with others on outward conformity. Depending upon your source, the Pharisees made anywhere from 500 to 1000 rules and laws out of the Ten Commandments. Jesus called them and their followers "whitewashed tombs" because they appeared righteous, but their hearts were hard.

This allows us to focus on the heart, not the structure. If all we want are people who say and do all the right things, then we do not need Christ. Jesus' mission focused on people's hearts because the heart is the source of our words and actions. Faith working through love is the highway to the heart.

Let us not be inflexible about our church ministries. By clutching onto and considering our programs as sacrosanct, we can erect a wall that separates us from God. Instead, let us create a household of God, committed to learning in life. I believe this gives us the best of what God offers! It enables us to keep our focus on Christ, while at the same time maximizing the potential for mature fruit.

As we delve into the actual rebuilding process, let us start by looking at the benefits. Setting our eyes on the benefits gives us motivation for thinking through and making changes in our ministries. Benefits help us to see that change is worth our time and effort.

Rebuilding The Household Of God

chapter 12

Throughout this book, I have maintained that God's church is a household of households. Each individual household might consist of a traditional family plus other members such as relatives, singles, single parents and their children, widows, orphans, and so on.

Looking at the church as a household focuses our attention on our similarities, not our differences. It challenges us to open our lives to others rather than slip into comfortable but exclusive groups that separate us from other members of the body of Christ. By building the church as a household, we ourselves grow. As we begin to influence, support, and guide people's lives through household ministry, we not only give to others but we learn many things as well.

The following graphic shows how household discipleship brings together all members of the church.

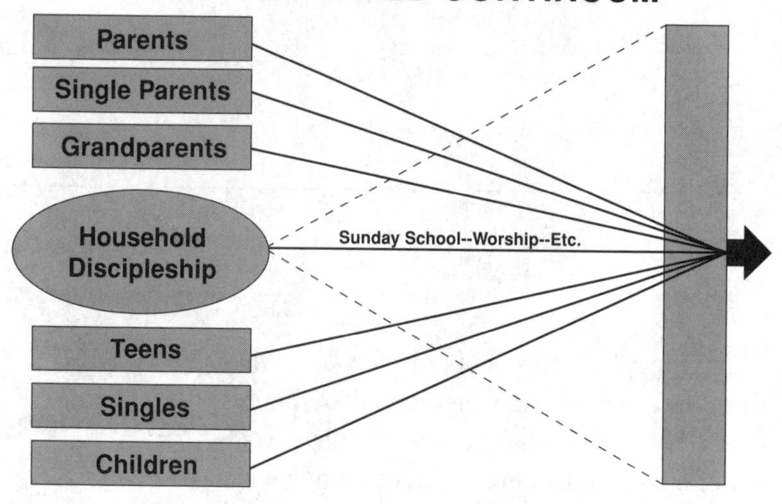

Benefits in Rebuilding God's Household

Let us now look at some of the benefits of taking a household approach to rebuilding God's church. Certainly there are many such benefits, but I will focus on eleven.

Benefit #1:

A household approach helps to heal the hurting, to clear up the confused, and to rebuild broken lives for victory.

Sin often leaves deep scars, which can take a long time to heal. By opening up our hearts, lives, and homes to others, we provide a haven for healing. Do you remember the story that Mark Hayes told in chapter one? His is a wonderful testimony of a single, divorced man who experienced how a household approach helped restore him to victorious living.

Benefit #2:
A household approach offers a natural outreach into the community.

Instead of relegating outreach to an evangelism program that meets on Wednesday nights, what if we viewed our everyday relationships with neighbors and other acquaintances as avenues for outreach? Evangelism involves more than presenting the gospel; it includes helping our neighbors carry in their groceries, mowing their lawn, sitting down and talking with them about what is on their mind, or sharing meals and activities with them. I know a group of households that regularly perform community projects at their own expense, such as planting flowers downtown. Their example invites questions from curious onlookers, which in turn enables them to share the gospel.

How much more initiative would our children have for outreach if it was a part of their everyday lives? If children grow up experiencing evangelism as a normal outgrowth of the Christian life, they will more likely make it a part of their own lives as adults.

How many more people would be open to the gospel if we lived it out before them? Did you come to Christ because someone handed you a tract, or because someone took the time to get to know you and introduce Christ through conversations and shared experiences over a period of time? Most people come to know the life-giving power of Christ through relationships. God may use tracts or other printed material to spark interest or kindle a flame, but God speaks most loudly through people during the "watering" process Paul describes in 1 Corinthians 3:6.

Many church programs focus on having a good time. While the Christian life is full of joys, there are many sorrows. Sometimes we must persevere through sorrows before we experience the joys! Jesus did not try to attract people by competing with the hedonism of His culture. He met people's needs, but He did not sugarcoat the gospel. In fact, He said, "The way is hard." If we approach nonbelievers with a desire to please God, we will be honest about the joys and sorrows of the Christian life. Then those whom we help bring to faith will better understand what the Christian life is really about. New believers will weather the storms of spiritual growth, resulting in strong leaders for future generations.

As neighbors and acquaintances see a household living in harmony, they may be responsive to the gospel because of our example. Not long ago, a single woman accepted Christ when a father and son from our church went to her home on an evangelistic visit. I asked her to write about the occasion and explain the impact this visit had on her.

Household-Style Evangelism

by Marcia McKelvey

On November 20, 1994, I was visited by a team of three people. Two of the members were household members, Mr. Lester Stadig and his son, Paul. The entire session was meaningful and resulted in my dedication of my life to Jesus. The single aspect of the visit which stands out in my mind, however, was the relationship between father and son Stadig.

I have no children but, nonetheless, have very strong convictions regarding the failure of households in raising children today. Perhaps because of my particular interest in children, I was particularly affected by what I observed, but I believe that the relationship would have a similar impact on anyone observing their relationship who was not used to seeing such openness between father and son. Four areas particularly struck me: (1) the fact that a teenager was at my house, apparently not under duress, on a Sunday night in a mission for God, (2) that the teenager was with his father and other adults, (3) the apparent routine aspect of the level of the communication they shared, and (4) the specific nature of the information shared.

Mr. Stadig easily shared his testimony in front of his son with no self-consciousness or embarrassment. It appeared to be information of which his son Paul was fully aware and accepting. This type of personal and religious communication appeared to be common between them. Additionally, Mr. Stadig shared information of a personal nature regarding personal sins in his life which I suspect few fathers share with their children. It also seemed to me that he was totally without desire to make himself appear "cool" to his son or a stranger. He also openly shared his feelings for his children and told me some of the ways he expressed them to his children as they were growing up. He appeared to experience pure, simple joy in their very existence and to have attempted to communicate that to them over the years. I can only look in from the outside, but it seems appropriate to say oh, what lucky children they are!

My assessment of what I observed is that this type of relationship between parent and child is extremely unusual. It is also what I consider representative of positive ideals, and appreciate increasingly that they are God's ideals for households. But whether an observer realizes at the time how much of what he observed in the household relationship actually is prescribed by God, I believe most would observe the relationship as positive and very, very unusual today. It therefore reflects very positively on Christians and should be of extremely positive value in attracting individuals to Christianity.

I believe that a good relationship between parent and child is very beautiful and relatively rare. If that relationship is observed in Christian households, it can only testify strongly for God.

I would like to add that this is the perspective not of a married woman, but that of a single woman.

A household approach not only enhances outreach to the local community but also to the global community. As Christians reach out to their neighbors with Christ's love, they naturally become more concerned for the salvation of souls worldwide. If the church concentrated on equipping its members to minister in their neighborhoods, we would all have a deeper appreciation for missions.

Benefit #3:
A household approach encourages hospitality as a means of serving one another in love.

Brotherly love is to be the hallmark of the church. In Romans 12:10-13 Paul tells Christians to pursue hospitality as a means of showing love. Many churches are rediscovering that hospitality provides the means for the multigenerational, heart-level discipleship we have discussed in this book.

In his book, *The Hospitality Commands*, Alexander Strauch writes,

> Unless we open the doors of our homes to one another, the reality of the local church as a close-knit household of loving brothers and sisters is only a theory. A cold, unfriendly church contradicts the gospel message. Yet unfriendliness stands out as one of the most common criticisms people have of local churches. It doesn't take people long to figure out that there is a "churchy" love among Christians that ends at the back door of the sanctuary or in the parking lot. It is a superficial, Sunday-morning kind of love that is unwilling to venture beyond the walls of the church building. Brotherly love, however, entails intimate relationship,

> care for one another, knowledge of one another, belonging together, and sharing life together. We cannot know or grow close to our brothers and sisters by meeting for an hour and fifteen minutes a week with a large group in a church sanctuary. The home is the ideal place in which to build relationships and closeness. (p. 17)

Hospitality is not difficult. It involves seeing the daily activities of the home as expressions of God's sovereign rule in our lives. In its simplest form, it is inviting people to our home for lodging, meals, activities, or just a visit.

Hospitality does not require having a home decorated by Martha Stewart or food prepared by the greatest chef in Paris. You do not even need Laura Ashley sheets on the guest bed. All you need is a heart brimming with love for the Lord Jesus Christ. Will hospitality always be convenient? Probably not. Is it time-consuming? Yes. But the benefits of hospitality are not just to those who receive it: the providers experience joy in return.

The relationship between love and hospitality is great. Our home is where we are most free and can enter into others' lives in a deeply personal way. When we learn hospitality at home, then that loving, caring attitude toward others will spill out into all avenues of human relationships.

For that reason, hospitality is also a dynamic tool for evangelism. The writer of Hebrews encourages Christians to show hospitality even to strangers (13:1-2). "Strangers" may be our neighbors whom we have lived next to for ten years but have never taken the time to get to know. They may be visitors to our church whom we invite over for Sunday afternoon lunch. The mailman, the news carrier, or passersby on a hot afternoon are people to whom we can show some measure of hospitality and thereby share the love of Christ. "Christian hospitality is truly distinctive from the world's practice of hospitality because it reaches out to unwanted needy people who cannot reciprocate" (Strauch, p. 24).

Benefit #4:
A household approach is well suited for listening to others and meeting their needs.

Jesus said, "Love your neighbor as yourself." It can be very difficult to fulfill this command if you and your neighbor have no regular one-on-one time together. Jesus went to the distressed and met their needs. He did not wait for them to come to Him. We must do the same for our neighbors.

The apostles stressed the importance of meeting the needs of widows and orphans in particular. (See James 1:27.) In the Roman world, these women and children had nowhere to turn for help and were often left to starve. In our day women have more options, but it is still extremely difficult for a single mother to raise her children and support them by herself. If she must work all day just to make ends meet, she will have little time or energy to build solid relationships with her children.

I remember meeting with a divorced mother who had an eleven-year-old son. The boy's father would have nothing to do with him. The mother worked diligently all day to support them both and earn enough money to put her child through Christian school. Because of the demands of work and school, their time together was limited to after-dinner homework sessions. I asked her what I could do to help. She very candidly stated that she would love to home-school her son because of the tremendous relationship benefits that would result, but she knew that such a dream was out of reach. Her heart's desire was to have a godly man come into her son's life and model Christ before him. She said, "I don't want him to repeat the failure of his father. I want him to be a godly husband and father. But for this to happen he needs to see it!"

She was not asking for the church to create a program with lots of fun activities. She simply wanted to be included in a household relationship. She knew that relationships were what she and her son needed in order to grow.

Benefit #5:
A household approach enables household members to grow together, to hold each other accountable, and to develop and live out a common vision.

When households learn and serve together, members achieve a greater level of accountability because they can more easily apply what they are learning to life situations.

I have found that I cannot hide in my household. There have been times when I avoided answering questions in Sunday school or held back singing in worship because I thought my household would say, "Who does he think he is?" They know how I live day to day and whether or not my participation is genuine. Thus when a household worships and studies together instead of attending separate programs, an important check is provided for everyone, especially the parents or other adult leaders.

When households learn and serve together, God often develops ongoing household ministries through shared vision. In my church, one of our elders is very involved in supporting our constitutional second amendment rights. This is a ministry because he is bringing biblical principles to bear upon our country's affairs. The son has caught his father's vision and has followed him into this work. The ministry will continue for another generation and more if the son passes this vision down to his own son.

Another family ministers together by serving as librarians at Harvester's Resource Center. While the parents are helping adults who visit the library, their children assist the visiting children. This working arrangement allows the librarian parents to teach their children by example what ministry is all about. The parents can monitor their children, and the children can watch their parents. At the end of the day, the family can talk together about their experiences.

Benefit #6:
A household approach provides the means for guiding new and young Christians through the struggles of Christian growth.

Peter describes new Christians as babies. Babies are not capable of feeding themselves, nor are they capable of making decisions. They need help. Paul describes himself as a "nursing mother" in 1 Thessalonians 2:7. This imagery emphasizes the nature of a ministry of ongoing care and direction that new and young Christians need in order to grow into mature leaders. A household approach allows for the continuous nurture of young Christians. Through such ministry we can end the spiritual immaturity that often defeats our churches.

Benefit #7:
A household approach helps us draw upon the wisdom of those who have gone before us.

Have you ever had the experience of learning something the hard way—you know, flubbing things up and wasting time and money? Perhaps your mistakes could have been avoided if you had allowed someone to share their wisdom on the matter.

Wisdom is vital to growth. Living in close relationship to others in a household makes it possible for everyone to share in and learn from the life experiences of others.

The elderly in particular are often an untapped spring of knowledge and wisdom. When they are brought into a household and made an essential part of it, they receive reciprocal benefits. They see their usefulness to others and are energized by being included in youthful living. Their stories of triumph and failure can inspire future generations to faith in God. Now more than ever, the younger generation needs to be encouraged and challenged to stay faithful to God because the world is telling them to trust only in themselves.

The elderly can help young people understand God's provision through tough times. They can also help moms and dads in practical ways around the home—the kind of help that was once provided through the "extended" household years ago. Grandparents used to be considered a valuable asset to a family. Not only could they help parents with teaching responsibilities, they could assist in meal preparation, maintenance, and hospitality. I know of a household that not only has a grandmother but also an older single woman living with them to help out with all of the duties. In return, these women receive the love of children and the assurance that they are not forgotten and have meaningful purpose.

The influence that my grandmother, Ethel Beatty, had on me was profound. She lived with us for her last thirteen years. She was born in 1899 and lived her first eighty-four years in Charlotte, North Carolina. Her testimonies of God's provision, repeated over and over, are forever etched in my mind and serve as a reminder of God's faithfulness. Had she not lived with us, I doubt that I would carry that indelible impression today.

During the Great Depression, my grandmother lived alone with her mother (her father was deceased) and was responsible for providing for her household. She was the secretary for a local cotton business. Due to some underhanded shenanigans by the owner, who absconded with all the money, she was out of work. The day after losing her job, she was walking down the street in downtown Charlotte when an owner of another cotton business, who also knew her, asked her why she was not at work. My grandmother told him the story and he immediately offered her a job. She was told to start the next day, which she happily did.

I can still hear my grandmother saying in her southern belle voice, "That was the Lord. The Lord provided me with that job. He knew that I needed it." At a time when people were losing their jobs, money, and homes, my grandmother was only out of work one day. God provided her material needs for the rest of her life through that position, as well as blessing her with a husband, and later a daughter—my mother. My grandmother will live in my memory as the greatest example of faith I have ever known. My family has always believed that her long life was a blessing from God because in her childhood she honored her father and mother. Her stories of how she would massage her mother's sore legs during illness for long hours night after night and her determination to provide for her mother has indeed encouraged me and my brothers and sisters to emulate her.

The fact that she lived with us for thirteen years as an integral part of our household also has a great deal to do with her longevity. She had a purpose for living. The physical help she provided my parents was incalculable. She lightened their load daily. On the very day she went into the hospital for the last time, she was helping my mom in the kitchen. She was also an enormous help to my brothers and sisters in raising their children. Hearing the wisdom from her life experiences and seeing how God worked through her made a lasting impression on my siblings and me and encouraged all of us to follow in her footsteps.

Herein lies the reciprocal benefit: she was needed and she

knew it. Even though she suffered with failing health in her last years, the fact that she was needed enabled her to keep her focus on God and not herself. She had a mission to complete, and her life was enriched with love and joy because of it.

No matter how old we are, we all need to be needed! When we know we are needed, we are more likely to give of ourselves sacrificially. There is a reason for our existence. We can affect the outcome of another life.

While this kind of relationship may seem out of reach for some now, it is never too late to start working toward this for our own family in the future. As parents we can inculcate this vision in our children and promise that we will be around to help them.

Benefit #8:
A household approach builds upon relationships that are long lasting and involve bearing with people through the seasons and trials of life.

Trials happen at all times, not just on Sunday mornings between nine and noon. It is during trials that people are most open to the life-giving truths of God's Word. Deep personal relationships developed through household ministry make counsel possible during these times.

Further, people are more open to correction, reproof, and training in righteousness when it comes from someone who has a history of loving commitment to them. I know of a pastor who, for this very reason, seeks to establish a relationship with his leaders before trying to counsel them on deep issues.

It is through endearing, loving relationships that we are able to model the grace and love of our heavenly Father to others. And people desperately need such modeling if they are to grow closer to God. They need to know that they are accepted as they are, warts and all, because of what Christ has already done for them. No level of involvement in a church program can replace this.

Benefit #9:
A household approach spreads leadership out over households instead of relying on a small team of overworked people.

In most churches, eighty percent of the work is done by twenty percent of the people. This is true because eighty percent of the people perceive that it is the "job" of the twenty percent to do the work. But for a household to succeed, each person must play a role. When pastors and elders work with household leaders, who in turn work with the members of their own households, this spreads leadership out. Doing this helps us build relationships, which in turn helps us keep our focus on Christ as the source of growth, not our own works.

Benefit #10:
A household approach allows more people to use their gifts in home settings where they can offer practical life guidance.

We mentioned earlier that church schedules and buildings can be confining for those whose gifts do not fit into the system. By giving people the freedom to develop relationships, instead of filling their time with programs, we make it possible for everyone in the church to give of their talents. For instance, a man who is a financial investment counselor can be challenged to mentor people who need his expertise. A person with the gift of teaching can be challenged to go into homes and help others learn how to teach. The sharing of gifts in this way outside of the church building provides a compelling testimony of the Father's love to unbelieving neighbors.

Benefit #11:
A household approach better prepares people for marriage.

A household approach to ministry enables young people to evaluate the characteristics of a potential marriage partner in the confines of safe, real-life relationships.

Before I married, the time I spent with the households in my church prepared me for the realities of married life better than any singles group ever could have. In fact, my whole approach to finding a wife changed as a result of those experiences. I began to look for a woman who knew how to manage a home and nurture children. I found these qualities in Leslee, who was involved with the household ministry of caring for out-of-wedlock babies. Dirty diapers, spit-up, crying babies, sick children, and disobedient children were a part of everyday life for her.

Something else I observed was her relationship with her father. How young women treat their fathers is usually a pretty good indication of how they will treat their husbands! (Likewise, how sons treat their mothers is a pretty good indication of how they will treat their wives.) I watched Leslee and her father intently as often as possible to determine exactly the nature of their relationship. Was she respectful of him? Was she loving? Was she interested? Did she take his word seriously? These were all qualities I wanted to be second nature to her because I knew she would treat a husband the same way.

Another characteristic I looked for was whether or not she knew how to solve problems biblically. Every marriage has problems. I wanted to marry a woman who knew how to pray and seek God's guidance through His Word on any issue that was causing conflicts. During our engagement, Leslee and I faced many tests together and we passed.

The rebuilding of God's household is a challenging but joyful task. This is not a pipe dream. It is achievable. In the next chapter, we will look at how your church can begin to implement a household approach.

Implementing a household approach begins with pulling together a team of people to research, plan and to appeal the leaders of your church. This is a crucial step that when done wrong has often led to failure. This chapter will give some suggestions for presenting this vision to your leaders and the congregation. You will also read about what a typical transition looks like and eight important foundation stones for transition.

Implementing A Household Approach

chapter 13

Implementing a household approach is not a process you should expect to happen quickly. Every church has a different character, personality, and direction, and therefore a "one size fits all" prescription will not suffice.

A myriad of factors, such as unity of the leadership, the size of the church, the number of age-segregated programs, or the age spread of the members, weigh into the decision of how to go about making changes. The majority of churches will apply these principles to already existing age-segregated ministries and will take a gradual approach; other churches will move rapidly. In either case, the place to start is with building a unified team. Those who have a desire to see this dream become reality—men, women, husbands, wives, pastors, and leaders—need to get together.

Warning! What you are about to do is strategic. It is very important that you handle this process humbly and lovingly. It has been my experience, and also that of others, that this initial phase is fraught with danger if you are not careful. The concept of making household relationships the foundation of church life is held to tenaciously by those who understand it. When others do not appreciate what you are trying to accomplish, the tendency can be to get defensive, angry, and bitter, or even to give up on the church. In such cases, what began as a loving, heartfelt appeal can quickly become a war that can end in ugly division.

Once you have called your team together, begin to discuss the vision, and pray and fast. (See Nehemiah 1:4; Daniel 6:10; Matthew 4:2.) For every minute you spend praying about the vision, spend five praying about your own attitude! Remember that many will reject the message if the messenger comes across in an angry or condescending manner. It is a loving, caring attitude—one that desires to see people's lives changed for the better—that will win those who are either "on the fence" or outright against you. The importance of attitude cannot be overstated.

Be careful to present the vision with patience and understanding. What may be clear to you may not be to some who are hearing this for the first, second, third, or even the fourth time. People need time to get used to new ideas. The best way to win their support is to nurture them along, not making them feel ignorant because they do not understand. There will be times when people will resist what you are proposing. Do not neglect these people. Meet with them and listen to their concerns. Do your best to assuage their fears and insecurities.

If there are those who ultimately reject your proposal, let them know you still love them, and try to keep communication open. Pray for them. Be careful not to gossip about them or ostracize them.

Clear Communication Is the Key to Success

Clear communication anticipates sources of friction and

seeks to alleviate others' fears. When you tell people you are going to experiment with a "household approach," some will automatically think this will mean the end of their favorite program, whether it be adult choir, youth group, or Sunday school. Brothers and sisters in Christ are not the enemy! Anticipate where the areas of friction are going to be. Plan how you are going to talk through those points and put people's minds at ease.

Clear communication dictates that people know what you are trying to do. If people think your goal is to end their favorite programs, then you are starting with an enormous handicap. Ending programs should not be your goal. Attacking the structures will not be nearly as effective as selling the benefits of the vision.

Clear communication involves defining your terms. One word may mean two entirely different things to two different people, depending on their church background and experience. For example, I find that the term "family approach" is often received negatively, because the word "family" is understood as too exclusive, meaning only "Dad, Mom, and the kids." However, the term "household approach" is more accurate, describing not just the nuclear family, but also singles, youth, single-parent households, the elderly, strangers, friends, and so on. The term "household" is more biblical, too. Word choices are very important, especially at a time in history when the meanings and connotations of words are changing rapidly.

Clear communication demands humility. When people ask questions you cannot answer, simply say so! Do not try to wing it. Affirm the importance of their question, then tell them you will research it and get back to them. I am always leery of people who appear to know everything—those zealots who make others feel as though they had better listen or get out of the way!

This attitude sears people's curiosity, creativity, and openness. People will find it easier to trust someone they perceive to be honest and real. Be open to the correction and suggestions of others. They need to be a part of this entire process! Let them dream, plan, and plant with you.

We must remember that lives are changed only through the power of Jesus Christ. Moving to a household approach will not change a person's heart any more than an age-segregated approach will. Jesus Christ changes hearts. I believe, however, that Jesus uses people in the process of changing hearts and that the household approach is a more effective way to build life-changing relationships in the church.

When I speak to groups, I exhort people to "start where you are, not where you want to be." Oftentimes, we see how far we are from where we think we should be and end up setting unrealistic goals. This breeds frustration, which can lead to bitterness and anger. To obviate this possibility, plan for a gradual implementation approach. This requires an accurate, honest appraisal of where you are starting from.

The Four-Fold Household Discipleship Vision As A Tool

In chapter six, we established that the church is God's household. Together, chapters eight, nine, and ten put forth the vision for household life, or ministry, which results in building leaders. This, the household discipleship vision, is strategic. It is very important that you and your team understand it and can communicate it clearly. The following "car" analogy will help you put it all together in your mind and will also provide a powerful presentation tool for you to use in selling the vision to others. Many audiences have responded quite well to this as an initial unifying foundation upon which we can begin to transform our churches.

"Generations"—the goal. When traveling to a destination, we must use the road.

God desires us to raise godly generations. Generations do not become godly overnight. It takes a lot of time, and a lot of God's grace to form them. It is like a long road trip! We must not become discouraged with "potholes" and "steep hills" that are a part of "the road" of preparing godly generations. By thinking long-term, we can avoid discouragement and finally arrive at the destination.

"Relationships"—the vehicle. A car carries us to a destination.

In His infinite wisdom, God designed relationships, beginning in the home, as the primary vehicle for working His plan over generations. In relationships there is love, accountability, protection, and encouragement. Relationships don't just happen. Relationships must be built through commitment to another person—a commitment that often involves great personal sacrifice. Satan understands this and from the beginning, in the garden of Eden, has attacked relationships. In the same way that a car protects us, only proven relationships that withstand the attacks of Satan will produce godly generations.

"Hearts"—the engine. The engine is the spirit that powers it all. An engine is what supplies the power to move the car down the road.

The engine is often referred to as the "heart" of the car. A car may look brand-new on the outside, but upon looking under the hood or taking the car for a drive, we can tell what the true condition of the engine is. When climbing the high mountains of life we will discern the true condition of the engine, whether it is a four-cylinder needing a valve job or an eight-cylinder strong enough to pull the Queen Mary.

God's goal is to transform our hearts into His image. If our goal is not to reach the hearts of our children, we will not produce faithful generations. It is very easy to be fooled about the true heart condition. Appearances may lead one to think that everything is OK in the heart when in actuality it is not.

"Everyday Life"—the road. The wheels work with the engine to move the car down the road. Tires allow the car to move down the road, to climb hills, to go through potholes, to swerve, turn, and basically maneuver the car. A good tire is necessary to keep a car on the road in bad weather. With bad tires, a blowout can occur and wreck the car.

The opportunities afforded by everyday life allow the parent to test the strength of their children's hearts in many different circumstances. In these situations the true heart condition can be known. Thus, the platitude "quality time is better than quantity time" is false. Teachable moments occur at many different times. The more time spent with a child will assure more opportunities to see inside the heart.

The picture of discipleship in the scriptures is that of relationships centered around everyday life—in most cases in the homes of believers. Discipleship is not a random event. God has established lines of authority, a basic structure in which discipleship can consistently and lovingly take place: the covenant household.

As I stated earlier, if you are a new church, your field is wide open for you to do what you want. If you are one of these, get started! Most of you, however, are in age-segregated program approaches, and the transition will take a little more time. Your church may choose, for example, to keep most of its current programs while introducing an age-integrated format at the same time.

A Typical Transition

While I was writing this chapter, I wanted to provide a single transitional model that any church could use as a guide. I labored and struggled to form a complete A-Z single model based on my work with hundreds of people from churches in forty-five states. I have worked with many different denominations, in churches of varying size and ministry emphasis. While there are some similarities in how each of these churches have implemented change, there is no single model that they all followed.

Then it dawned on me that this is indeed the beauty of this whole approach! There does not need to be a single model that works for everybody. This approach is adaptable to any church, in any denomination. The truth of this fact confirms what matters most: it is the Holy Spirit, working in the hearts of His people, that provides the model. This is a movement not of human effort but of the Spirit of the living God.

With this in mind, what follows is a list of common steps that many churches have followed to implement change.

Once the team has presented the vision, the first step for a typical church is to begin an age-integrated Sunday school class.

Such a class includes singles, single-parent households, nuclear households, elderly, youth, and so on. (In the next chapter I have a few interviews with pastors who have found this to work quite well.) Adding or replacing a class in the roster on Sunday morning is an easy change and allows the team to begin applying these principles in the church's meeting place. This offers a dual benefit. First, it relieves those who want to move ahead, and second, it gives time for others to observe this vision being implemented gradually. Thus, bridges are built and strengthened between leaders and members of the church.

There are three benefits to an age-integrated Sunday school class. First, generations become linked. Very often the class is taught by a head of household, a husband-and-wife team, a single, a grandparent, or even a whole household. Allowing entire households to lead gives young people the opportunity to develop their leadership skills. It also broadens everyone's view of leadership. Leaders are not just the preacher and his staff.

Second, the content is more interesting and motivational. The vast majority of curriculum used is homemade. People are more apt to teach from their life experiences. Their unique personalities, gifts, goals, dreams, and struggles become apparent to others.

Third, household relationships are developed outside of the class. Every Sunday school teacher wants to see his or her hard work actually stick with people and help them grow. What is taught does not stop at the door to the classroom. Very often relationships blossom outside of the class as a result of what is taught in Sunday school. For instance, a father may teach a class on how to study the Bible but finds that the single person sitting in the last row comes up to him and asks him to mentor him in how to study the Word. The resulting relationship allows the father to help the single develop into a well-rounded, mature adult.

Over time, the people who come to these classes form small groups (or cell groups, as some call them) for further edification through the week. The relationships that grow soon begin to season other people and ministries in the church.

A typical church will begin to see changes in other areas of ministry as well. For example, the church's youth ministry will begin to see the involvement and influence of parents. Parents may attend youth ministry meetings in order to work more closely with youth leaders. In such cases, youth ministry is transformed. Some churches eventually drop youth group altogether because the needs of the youth are being met in household and church relationships.

Church leaders begin asking a lot of questions about ministry. This is a period of study and discovery. Many get together and begin studying these issues more deeply, seeking to learn how to apply these principles to all ministries. As a result, basic common themes and vision develop between ministries.

Households begin staying together, and more households form. Singles spend more time with households or even live with them. People go out of their way to help each other and share their lives. Children and youth mature earlier and rise up to leadership.

Almost without exception, churches see fathers take more of a leadership role, not just in their households but also in church ministry. Homes and neighborhoods are rediscovered as bases for ministry.

In many churches, there may be an overall reduction in traditional church-sponsored activities, but these are replaced by more effective heart-level relationship-based ministry, which yields greater spiritual fruit.

In summary, the transition deepens relationships with God and others and broadens ministry by reaching outside the church and into the everyday lives of hurting people. Lives are reconnected and the power of the gospel flows like blood through the veins of God's children. Shared vision, commitment, and love for each other become the hallmark of this church. This is ministry that brings salt and light into the harvest fields.

Laying the Foundation

Now that we have looked at some typical transitional steps, let us talk about laying the foundation needed to get this new approach off to a strong start. Think of each of these as stones upon which we step on our journey from the traditional approach to the household approach.

Foundation Stone #1:
Think in terms of the gospel.

No approach to ministry can do what the gospel already does. To quote my good friend Ben Taylor, "Faith is not a formula." We cannot substitute faith with our best efforts. We are completely acceptable to Christ on the basis of His work alone. There is nothing we can do to be more acceptable to Him. We therefore have the freedom to live according to what is already ours through Christ. Our ministry relationships are then real opportunities to freely grow in grace.

Foundation Stone #2:
Be flexible.

The principle of flexibility is found in 1 Corinthians 9:22, where Paul says, "...I have become all things to all men that I may by all means save some." When one stops to consider God, He is very flexible in this area of our methods for working out ministry. Flexibility is closely associated with creativity. Being made in God's image, we are creative individuals. God wants us to use our creativity to serve Him.

We need to be flexible in two ways. First, we should avoid thinking of our church programs—whether they are age-segregated or household-based—as non-negotiable. Not everyone will agree on what to do about programs anyway, so we need to be willing to modify our ideals accordingly.

Second, we should be flexible in our time frame for implementing this approach. More than likely, it will take longer than we want or expect. We must not grow weary, though, remembering that God is sovereign and He will accomplish His work in His time.

Foundation Stone #3:
Be willing to learn.

My father always said that life is a process of learning how to learn. Since we all want quick solutions in life, this seems rather unpalatable. But making the transition toward a household approach demands that we learn. Most churches that succeed have leaders who are constantly reading, thinking, and reevaluating what they do and how they do it. Applying these truths to our postmodern times is difficult and challenging and demands continual study and refinement.

A willingness to learn also necessitates a willingness to fail. We have to proceed humbly, acknowledging our own weaknesses and prepare to experience failures. We need not fear failure; it is through failure that we learn to walk more closely with God.

Foundation Stone #4:
Think in terms of the heart-level relationships.

The heart must be our goal, just as it is Christ's goal. We must evaluate the effectiveness of our ministry not by numbers and money but by the condition of people's hearts. Instead of building activities around attendance, we need to build activities around relationships that get to the heart. Throughout the Bible we see people who did the right things, but their hearts were far from God. We must ask, are people growing spiritually in their love and service of the Savior? Are we helping to build household relationships, or are we building bigger and "better" programs?

Foundation Stone #5:
Be realistic about your place in relationships.

We must beware not to take on unbiblical responsibility for someone's life. We are training people to be healthy, mature believers. We cannot do what only God can do. When a child or disciple just does not seem to get it or even resists, we cannot make them do what is right. We must pray for God to change their hearts; then we must love them and enter into the sanctification process with them. Some have forgotten the latter requirement and have become heavy-handed and manipulative. That is to be avoided at all costs. Showing love toward one another is crucial.

Foundation Stone #6:
Be prepared for growth and division.

Many churches have tried the cell-group approach only to find groups getting too big and unwilling to divide so that others can be included. This has led to ingrownness in some churches. There is always a tendency to stay in our own comfort zone. God calls us out of our comfort zones that we may grow in grace and faith.

Foundation Stone #7:
Be committed to the multi-generational growth of leaders.

The acid test of leadership is not when the current generation proves faithful but rather when future generations prove faithful. A common thread through all ministry should be the equipping of leaders with a vision and the tools to prepare others to be leaders. Moreover, a true leader is not one who sees his role restricted to an office or position. He views leading as an all-encompassing responsibility that extends into all corners of life and relationships beginning in the home.

Foundation Stone #8:
Be willing to grow into ministry.

In other words, do not be afraid to start small. Many people report that starting small gives them great freedom in implementing their vision. It really makes a difference simply to stop, take a deep breath, accept God's providence for where they are, and be willing to start at that point. Better to start small and enjoy great success than to promise grandiose success and end up gaining nothing. Be prepared for God's providence to alter your plans! Remember Romans 8:28-29: "All things work together for good to those who love God."

As You Begin to Build

As you begin to build on the foundation and make this transition, keep in mind the following teaching points to help you stay focused and reach your goal.

Teach household leaders how to teach.

In many homes it will be important to teach the parents how to model the Christian life at home.

Teach principles that can be lived.

Teaching may need to be modified somewhat to help children understand the material. At home, during the week, the parent illustrates the principles in life. Therefore, teaching parents how to teach is one of the primary goals.

Christian teaching is often cerebral, theological, and abstract. As we integrate the ages together, it forces us to make our ideas simple and concrete. This is good discipline. If we can make theology and doctrine understandable to a young person, it is more likely that we truly grasp what we are talking about. Jesus used concrete objects and ordinary events to teach abstract truths. His simple examples provided an understandable way to make truth accessible and easy to remember.

I still remember a children's sermon from over ten years ago when the pastor used his wedding ring, focusing on how round and "unending" it was, as an object lesson to represent the never-ending nature of marriage and our relationship with God. If you think that pastors only plan children's sermons for children, think again! The principle clearly works for adults as well.

Teach truth that lives.

Sadly, the life-giving truths of God's Word have suffered rigor mortis in many of our churches. People may have memorized many Bible verses and have heard the familiar stories repeatedly, but they often fail to relate these truths to their everyday lives. We need a resurrection of truth from lifeless words on a page to deeply meaningful, challenging, guiding nuggets of wisdom for our lives.

For example, what does it mean that God is our Father? We address God as our Father in prayer quite often, but does it mean more to us than an introduction to prayer? Could it be that God wants us to know Him as One who loves us, cares for us, provides us assurance, security, and is deeply committed to what is best for us? I know that because He is my father, He will not turn me away and will give me only good things that will draw me closer to Him. Understanding God as a father helps us to understand who He is, how He relates to us, and most importantly how we are to relate to Him.

The direction that He gives us for living cannot be relegated to a twenty-step process that we can do all on our own. We need Him to walk us through the paths of darkness and light. As He does this every day, we learn where He wants us to go, what He wants us to do, and how He wants us to get there. His plan and purpose for our lives becomes evident. And when we step off the path and wander into the enticements of the world, He corrects us in love and brings us back to His path. We need not fear that He will leave us or forsake us. We are His adopted children who have an everlasting inheritance.

As leaders learn to more effectively teach these truths, the wonderful thing is that they learn these relational truths themselves! These are the questions people ask in everyday life. The answers we give them will either give spiritual life or crush it.

Some Good News About Converting Existing Programs

Programs can be transformed and used as opportunities for household units to learn, work, and serve together. In these programs, issues can be addressed that were once addressed through the individual age-segregated group programs. This pattern of leadership will especially require fathers' involvement as a way to build leadership skills in the men.

Programs that target individual groups can still maintain the individual focus but should be carried out within the context of household units.

We must remember that many of these programs meet needs that are the result of the breakdown in the family, or have in effect replaced or infringed upon the role of the father as head of the household. By keeping households together, and building up fathers, we can avoid the potential trap of replacing them.

You have the vision, the team and a lot of energy. How might some of your current ministries look when household principles are applied? This chapter contains some ideas from other churches who have made transitions in key ministries. Some very unique examples are provided to help stir your own creativity.

From Seperation to Integration

c h a p t e r 14

How Each Individual Program Can Reflect a Household Approach

Sunday morning worship is the cornerstone for ministry in any church. Applying a household approach here can be quite simple. To begin with, make it a pattern that households sit together. Church leaders can select from within the congregation to offer public prayers of confession. Focus on encouraging parents to share about scriptures and trials and victories. Having households stand up and give testimony encourages other adults and children to take on spiritual leadership of their households.

Have fathers, singles, and even mature teenage boys deliver brief messages as a way of developing their leadership capacities.

Make sermons very practical. Address topics such as relationships, dating and courtship, discipline, how to prioritize, how to develop life vision, choosing a vocation, serving in the community, etc. Care must be taken that the worship service remains worshipful of God. This requires constant vigilance.

For Communion: have elders serve heads of households the elements, who then serve them to their own households.

"Sermon Notes"

A.W. Tozer once said, "Bible exposition without moral application raises no opposition. It is only when the hearer is made to understand that truth is in conflict with his heart that resistance sets in. As long as people can hear orthodoxy divorced from life, they will attend and support churches and institutions without objection. On the other hand, the man who preaches truth and applies it to the lives of his hearers will feel the nails and thorns. He will lead a hard life, but a glorious one."

The life-application oriented sermon is almost extinct in the church today. Perhaps this is why only nineteen percent of adults say that they learn a lot from the sermon (*Why Nobody Learns Much of Anything at Church: And How to Fix It* by Thom and Joani Schultz, p. 9).

I know one pastor who prepares sermon outlines that are often two to three single-spaced 8 1/2 x 11 pages in length. I have had the opportunity to visit his worship service on a few occasions and see for myself the difference this made in discussion, encouragement, and application. Taking biblical principles and making application brings theology (God's principles for living) to life.

Another pastor I know actually discusses the sermon with his households (in place of Sunday school) immediately after the worship service. During this time, he discusses application so that they can apply what they learned to everyday life. Daily application would do wonders for sermons that many people endure on Sunday mornings!

Sunday School

Focus on teaching households as units. Seek to have whole households (mothers, fathers, sons, daughters, singles, youth) take turns teaching a class. Church leaders would do well to get to know the households and channel them to certain classes. Use analogies from life. Teaching as a unit provides an incredible visual testimony to visitors and helps relationship building.

Classes should be very practical. Address head-on topics that people face each day, such as relationships, finding purpose in life, setting priorities, developing vision, how to choose a doctor, debt, living on less, and so on.

Where possible, tie Sunday school themes into other ministry opportunities that take place on Sunday or Wednesday evening, such as children's ministries.

Switch Sunday school with the morning worship service. There are several advantages, including starting Sunday with the household together. This will alleviate the waiting, hectic scurrying, circus-like atmosphere that exists in smaller churches between Sunday school and the worship service. It is important to note that this is usually the first impression visitors get when they walk through the door!

Holding the worship service first will also increase Sunday school attendance because people will already be there.

One final improvement may be to consider eliminating nursery during Sunday school. (More on this in a moment.)

Church Households That Work

Some churches, like Victory Baptist, pastored by Steven Ong, in Greeley, Colorado, have written their own curriculum, called Scripture Activities for Household Enrichment (S.A.F.E.). They have only one Sunday school class. Among ten curriculum units are included: Heroes of the Faith, People in Proverbs,

Christian Armor, Pastoral Epistles, 1 Peter, and Hebrews.

How it works

Households meet together on Sunday morning for an opening session to sing and receive instructions (5-15 minutes). The group then disperses into household units to read and discuss the scripture lesson. It is important to note that households adopt visitors and other members of the church and include them in these activities.

The groups begin their study with the prayers of the parents and children. Then they work together on different Bible projects. These sessions are led by the head of the home (30-45 minutes). Sometimes it is appropriate to put one or more households together, but in such a case only one head of the home is teaching. Households continue to work on the projects at home during the week.

Why it works

Households become united as they pray and work together. As children see the head of the home teaching and living the principles, they are encouraged in their own character development. The program uses mutual accountability among the members as each one applies spiritual principles to daily living.

Victory member Becky Martin has found that this approach adds "true depth" to ministry. "I have had to work through many obstacles in my life due to divorce. Seeing other families 'walk the talk' has helped me overcome obstacles and see how I can more effectively help others." Becky sees this integrated approach as being essential to people like her who have suffered broken relationships, because it equips her "not to repeat the same failures."

Another approach

Calvary Worship Center in Port St. Lucie, Florida has made some incredible strides in the area of Sunday school.

In 1991 the leaders began to see that their Sunday school teachers were burning out. Some were dropping out of the ministry and the church altogether. After six months of intensive prayer, the leaders became convicted that splitting up the household into separate classes on Sunday mornings was having a negative impact. They discovered it was being counterproductive in developing a spiritual head of household.

They decided to eliminate Sunday school altogether and instead equip parents to teach at home. (They instituted a family-style praise and worship time during the former Sunday school hour). So every Wednesday evening for a period of one month, the staff met in the homes of their members to describe this new vision. Pastor Bob Roach, who was the head of the project, said, "Many of the parents were frustrated with the way they lived. They were frustrated with the way their households were, and they were looking for answers of how to bring their households together. They wanted to do it God's way. There was something in their hearts that wanted more of a relationship with their children."

They knew that they needed a two- to three-month transition plan. The first stage of this plan was to meet with their Sunday school teachers and share the vision. They became their "home Sunday school" teachers. Their purpose was to help fathers establish a family altar in the home. Initially, the church purchased age-segregated curriculum for each father to use with his household. But this obviously proved to be too expensive and created frustration. "We learned that you can't set up Sunday school in the home," Bob recalls.

So Bob sat down at his computer and wrote a curriculum

that involved participation from all individuals of the household. After six years, he has written three tracks of curriculum: Doctrines of the Faith, Raising Children, and Household Worship.

The leadership realized that they may lose some people over this but were prepared to accept the loss because they knew it was what God wanted them to do. (In the end, they only lost one family.) When they started this new approach in 1991, they had fifty households involved. In five years God multiplied the participation from fifty to 280. Calvary now sends the curriculum to fifteen different churches nationwide.

The benefits of this approach include a more effective evangelistic impact upon the community. Households witnessing to other households have brought whole households into the church that otherwise would not be there. It has brought the household together in unity, stability, and around the things of God. Within the first month of implementing this approach, twenty-eight children made professions of faith. Bob reports that some households on the brink of divorce were turned around as they came together in the home each day.

One such family came one Sunday and the father came forward to rededicate his family to Jesus Christ. At the time the family was in the midst of a divorce. Unknown to anyone in the church, the family was deeply engrossed in a cult that kept them out from midnight to three in the morning three nights a week. Through this association, the father had become a transvestite, had changed his name from Marty to Mary, and had planned a sex-change operation. His sons had developed mental and emotional problems and were on mind-altering drugs. Their house was full of all sorts of transvestite- and homosexual-oriented magazines, and the family operated a cult-related Internet bulletin board.

Over a four-year period, Bob worked with this family, helping them, among other things, purge their home of satanic materials. The real turning point came, however, when they replaced the worship of Satan in the home with Calvary's "Family Altar" home Sunday school program. God used this "household approach" to help heal the wounds in this family by uniting them around God's Word and worship every day. Now, four years later, the father is one of the church's cell-group leaders, and all except one of the sons (who is still unsure) are serving the Lord. The family bulletin board that once introduced people to Satan now introduces hundreds of people to Christ!

Clearly the greatest benefit of this approach is what it has done for its fathers. In particular, fathers have taken on a deeper understanding and commitment to leading their wives and children in the home. Not surprisingly, this has spilled over into other branches of ministry at Calvary, with more fathers taking on the mantle of leadership.

Living Our Faith Before a Watching World

As households begin to "gel" and relationships begin to grow, the body is not the only group to be blessed. The world benefits too from a more pervasive witness, because the Christian relationship is best represented by how we live, not only by what we say. Telling others of our hope in Christ through trials and prosperity revitalizes evangelism in a number of ways.

First, by keeping households together and encouraging them to witness to neighbors and friends through their daily activities, we make living the gospel an inclusive and encompassing activity. Instead of a once-a-week "cold turkey" effort, we stress discipleship as the end goal in evangelism. Jesus said in Matthew 28:19 that we are to "make disciples." Someone praying to receive Christ is only a small part of discipleship. A good question to ask someone entering an evangelism class is, "How many people are you prepared to disciple?"

If we do not see discipleship as the big picture in evangelism, we compartmentalize our witnessing efforts and forget how evangelism is tied to how we live every day. When the gospel is presented outside of this framework, people may see a decision to receive Christ as purely mental or emotional. Hence, we spend a lot of time sowing tares.

One example of the impact that households ministering together can have is seen in one of my own church's households. God used a ten-year household-to-household relationship to bring a man and his family to the Lord. Through the combination of their faith and life, God used the May household to bring the Pejacks to a point of true understanding of Christianity. As a result, Frank and his wife are clearly committed, growing, and contributing to the church community. The discipleship process began before Frank became a Christian. Conversion was simply an outgrowth of a discipleship relationship. But it was Frank seeing God work in David May's household through many circumstances that led him to make a profession of faith.

Households working together to serve their community can have quite an impact for the gospel. Joe Camilleri's church in Rochester, New York, lives the gospel before community leaders through service projects. Below is a testimony of how the gospel has gone forth through these opportunities.

> Many inroads have been made in our community here in Rochester, New York. The responses of politicians and community leaders say best the kind of impact our households are having: at a recent clean-up of a historical site, the president of the historical society, who is a city schoolteacher remarked, "I have never seen families

like this in my life." She noted that the most overpowering impression that had been made on her was that "they are so happy!" I had to keep myself from jumping up and down and shouting with happiness when she stated that "they are like old-fashioned families!" After allowing me to explain the biblical design for a household, and that freedom from the pressures of evil allow this happiness to exist, she responded, "Yes, that's it!"

At a recent meeting with many community leaders present, testimony was given on behalf of that project for ten minutes...one commented that "these are the kind of people who will change the world." While our young people were serving refreshments at a council meeting, one of our men was able to explain the gospel when asked, "How do you explain these children!"

Children's Ministries

The Achilles' heel of many children's ministries has been the lack of parental involvement. If we are going to be faithful to our principles about parental authority and responsibility, and if we are truly going to see what is taught lived out in the lives of the children, then parents must be involved. Often what is taught is not known or understood by the parents. It may not even agree with their goals, so there is no reinforcement at home. Thus we produce little "hearers" and not "doers" of the Word (James 1:22).

Over time, God can bring synergy between boys' and girls' ministries. Since many households have children in both, it is not hard to put the two together and separate only for occasional gender-specific activities. Study character traits with the children and tie the teaching thematically to the children's Sunday school curriculum. Consider meeting on a weekday at a location other than the church, where real-life activities can be enjoyed.

Example of Transforming a "Little Boys" Ministry

Today's popular children's ministries separate children from their parents. Harvester had such a ministry that focused on boys. When I was given that ministry in 1993, I scrapped it and started over. I threw away all of the curriculum and built upon the basic premise that fathers should be with their sons, and in fact should share responsibility for teaching such a class. The idea was to have a father and his son teach the other fathers and their sons by simply relaying a relationship activity that they had engaged in during the week. The following describes in more detail what our goals for fathers and sons were, as well as how we set out to accomplish them.

OBJECTIVES: "To turn the hearts of fathers back to the children" (Luke 1:17). "Now may the God of hope fill you with all joy and peace in believing, that you may abound in hope by the power of the Holy Spirit" (Romans 15:13). "And these words which I am commanding you today, shall be on your heart; and you will teach them diligently to your sons and shall talk of them when you sit in your house and when you walk by the way and when you lie down and when you rise up" (Deut. 6:5-7).

GOALS: To help fathers develop and apply a vision which dictates that every activity with their sons is an opportunity to disciple them to fulfill God's covenant promise for leadership and evangelism.

To help fathers grow in their understanding of covenant education by integrating biblical and academic principles in real-life situations where they can teach their children.

To help young boys understand and appreciate the importance of the father-son relationship.

To help young boys develop and commit to living the discipleship vision for their children when they become fathers, thus assuring the passage of the covenant to future generations.

To help fathers and sons grow in their understanding of God's attributes and character and how to apply this knowledge to bring others to Christ.

To have a practical covenant education witness to our church and the community.

To help fathers and sons see everyday activities as opportunities to present the gospel.

To give children the opportunity to practice speaking before a group.

STRATEGY: The Fathers and Sons ministry will provide a forum and practical encouragement for fathers and sons to share with other fathers and sons specific activities in which they have participated together involving the use of predetermined criteria.

PLANS: Every Sunday night that Fathers and Sons meets, a father-and-son team will present an activity they have worked on together. The father and son will explain how they met the seven criteria mentioned in the next section. Father-son teams in the room are encouraged to ask questions about the presentation. These teams will be scheduled for presentations.

CRITERIA: Points to be included in the presentations:

1. What was the God-related objective?

   Since God's attributes are revealed in every aspect of His creation (Romans 1:20), what does this topic teach us about God?

2. What is the life-related objective?

   Since God commands our dominion over creation (Gen. 1:28), how does this topic prepare one to govern social relationships and/or the physical creation?

3. How did you apply areas of discipline such as math, English, science, etc.?

4. What did your use of math, or English, or science teach you about God?
5. Bring visual aids (i.e., demonstrate what you did if possible).
6. For fathers to comment on: What one new thing did you learn about your son that you didn't know before?
7. For sons to comment on: What one new thing did you learn about your father that you didn't know before?

Once a month, a father and son will be selected by the leader to present a report to the congregation on Sunday morning. Every father- and-son team will have an opportunity to report. (The long-range objective is to see this new format bridge over to include Fathers and Daughters.)

CONSIDERATIONS: Fathers and Sons meetings will include fathers with boys age five through sixth grade. We will include boys who do not have a father by having father-son teams "adopt" them.

For Churches with Sunday Evening Meetings

One idea would be to use Sunday evenings as a time for households to get together and share spiritual gifts and abilities.

The leaders of one church pair households together. The two households meet and discuss what gifts and abilities they want to "exchange." Every individual, including the youngest children participate in this. Over a six-month period, the households get together in all sorts of different everyday life settings and equip each other through teaching and modeling. In some cases, they are taught by one of the children! After six months, the households would rotate.

Another idea is to free up some or all of the Sunday evenings so that households can actually rest on Sunday, or develop relationships within themselves, with others in church or their neighbors.

Youth Ministry

As we saw earlier in this book, typical youth ministry is the result of erroneous thinking that saw no benefit in age-integrated relationships. There is need to restore primary relationships, namely that of parents to their teenage children. Youth ministry can be a catalyst for this. At my church, we have made several changes in our approach to youth ministry. Luke Godshall, our youth ministry leader is married and sees his responsibility as being primarily a resource to parents anyway, and he likes it that way. His whole family is involved in the activities. Youth leaders often become surrogate parents, which can actually perpetuate problem relationships in the home. Working with parents helps to alleviate this possibility.

Most youth activities involve the youth and their households.

Actually, we have integrated many youth and adult activities in an effort to keep the household together. In Sunday school, for instance, youth and adults attend the same classes. We found that purely age-integrated classes were successful with youth and parents who already had good relationships. However, those youth who came to church without their parents struggled or dropped out. A youth/adult class that appeals more to youth has helped to hold those youth who we would otherwise lose while trying to assimilate them into household relationships.

Cell Groups

Many churches have small groups called "cell groups" or "care groups" that meet during the week. These groups can be dynamic tools in building nurturing relationships.

Small groups can be a better starting point where modeling

and accountability can be introduced. As relationships become the main mode of ministry, all major equipping activities should eventually occur through them. By focusing on their own neighborhoods, cell groups can encourage and oversee outreach.

Without any connection to other ministries, cell groups, however, are viewed as just another program or weeknight to be away from home and have therefore become lost in the helter-skelter of everyday life.

When the Harvester leadership started our Care Groups, they decreed that ministries could not meet regularly on weeknights, so that emphasis could be placed upon involvement in our Care Groups.

Many of our Care Groups start off with a twenty-minute singing and sharing time that includes the children. After this time, the children are taken into another room while the parents receive uninterrupted instruction. As children get older and better behaved they stay with the adults the entire time.

A key ingredient to re-tooling small groups is holding out a vision for the importance of household relationships and God's design for scriptural leadership.

Small groups are not an end but the beginning. All nurture and examination cannot occur on Wednesday nights! Freedom to do the Acts 2 "one-anothering" and pursue hospitality should occur throughout the week. Relationships and ministry should blossom from the groups. Great care should be taken not to stifle hospitality, and it may just be that regular cell group meetings should occasionally "free wheel" to allow for one-anothering.

We must put a priority on communicating this vision of household nurture and accountability. Household heads need to set biblical priorities and guard time together, and channel more of it toward ministry purposes.

As we develop the household-based vision in our members

by applying the principles in this plan, we will see change. As more mature fruit is put on display, more people will realize what they are missing!

Thoughts on Nursery

You might be thinking, with all of this integration, what do we do about unruly children, who seem to make nursery a given?

There is the issue of crying babies, and then there is the issue of young children who are capable of doing better. In the former case, providing a nursery is helpful. But in the latter case, consider if we are always offering an "out" for parents who have undisciplined children, what incentive are we offering them to discipline? Many young children can sit quietly through a worship service when they know it is expected of them. Although it is never pleasant to deal with the distraction of an undisciplined child, we must bear with these parents while they struggle to gain control (Galatians 6:2).

Providing a nursery or "children's church" for older, chronically unruly children can and often does take the impetus off of training the parents to train their children, because it tries to do it for them.

In Harvester's case, we have set up what we call the "Titus 2:4 Nursery." The objective of this nursery is not to provide a haven for unruly children. Rather, a more spiritually mature woman attends to the nursery and works with mothers who bring their unruly children in during a worship service. The children cannot stay without a parent staying with them.

The logical progression to train children is first, control during family devotions, second, control within a larger Care or Cell Group, then church classes and worship. Church is not a training ground, it is evidence of training elsewhere.

Home-Education Ministries

Some churches already have home-education ministries. These ministries, when properly developed, can help move the church toward a household approach.

Because all parents are home-educators, these ministries can provide resources for all household leaders. A well-equipped resource center can help more than just home-schoolers, since many resources focus on parenting issues, relationship issues, and practical application of faith.

Home-schoolers have contacts with many speakers who can teach, challenge, and encourage leaders. Home-school support groups can offer a platform to teach on certain life issues, such as setting priorities, establishing a budget, discipline, relationship issues, learning how to study the Bible, discipleship, living within your means, and so on.

By focusing on such heart-related issues, Harvester's home-education ministry has benefited singles, youth, single-parent households, divorcees, couples, and the elderly.

Missions and Evangelism

At Harvester, we have applied household principles to our missions trips to come up with another unique household ministry. Recently, we sent a group of families to Atlanta, Georgia, to help a local ministry renovate an apartment complex located in a drug-infested section of town. While fathers and their sons rebuilt walls, re-carpeted floors, painted, and performed other tasks, mothers and their daughters prepared meals and taught a vacation Bible school to the neighborhood children. Everybody was pitching in! Parents and children were able to serve and learn together, and neighbors were given a picture of what the gospel can do to build healthy families.

Keeping families together is a theme in Harvester's evangelism program as well. Families are encouraged to take the class and go out on evangelistic visits together. In a previous chapter, I relayed the testimony of one single woman who was visited by one of our families. The impact of a father and son simply being together elicited a very positive response.

Total Immersion

Stewart Jordan, pastor of Redeemer P.C.A church in Madison, Alabama, has started a new church based entirely upon household principles. They have no age-segregated ministries. They focus on Sunday morning worship and building of the leaders through hospitality. Stewart reports that he sees hospitality as more and more the key to developing a household-based ministry. He adds, "If the church is practicing hospitality, then there is no need for other ministries."

Stewart began meeting with five men for lunch on Fridays. During that time he helped the men understand Genesis so that they could teach it to their households, providing them with specially prepared outlines to help them teach.

In February 1996 when Stewart started his church, he had fourteen households. Now, a little more than two years later, there are twenty-seven households, including three single adults, two single mothers, and two mothers whose husbands do not attend. The singles and single mothers joined because they realized what they needed could best be delivered through household relationships.

Unique Household Ministries

F.I.S.H.

One of Harvester's households has a unique ministry called F.I.S.H., which stands for Fellowship of International Students and Hosts. Dave and Bev Froberg have always had a burden for foreign students, especially those from China, who come to the United States to study. In order to more effectively minister to these people, they relocated to be close to the George Mason University campus. On every Friday night they invite the students over for fellowship. Dave and Bev include their three young children in the activities. Very often, they invite other church members over to their house to share with the students an interest, vocation, or an aspect of American culture. As the households share, biblical principles are effectively woven through the presentations to show how Christianity is a faith that affects all areas of life. This household-based ministry is an excellent example of household-based outreach for several reasons:

The goal is to build relationships. It involves the household as a unit, under the leadership of the father, in the home (so that people can observe biblical living), reaching out into the community through hospitality. Church members are invited to come and share their gifts and interests in the context of biblical principles. This provides flexibility for various gifts to be exercised and the gospel to go forth.

"Show and Tell"

Grace Bible Fellowship in Walpole, New Hampshire, has had some innovative programs over the years. One of them is called "Show and Tell." Fathers choose a project that they want to work on with one of their children. The project must have a God-related objective and a life-related objective. The God-related objective involves showing how godly character qualities are revealed in the project. The life-related objective involves communication and relationship skills. Only the fathers are allowed to work with the children on these projects, which are then presented on Sunday morning after the worship service. On the Sunday I visited, eight fathers and their children had projects to share.

One father and son reported on a project involving their garden. They planted pumpkins at various locations with varied sunlight and moisture. The little boy lugged a humongous pumpkin about half his size up front and, with the help of his father, placed it on the table. Next to it, they put a small, sickly pumpkin. I remember the God-related objective of the project. Just as proper light and water is necessary for pumpkins and other fruits and vegetables to grow, so it is that we as Christians need the light and living water of God's Word in order to grow spiritually. In this presentation and others, I was excited by what I saw but did not hear: the close relationship these fathers had built with their children.

Scripture teaching would be so much more effective if we would simply couple it with objects in everyday life that surround us. Imagine what an encouragement it would be for parents to see other parents stand up on Sunday morning and present a report that showed relationship-building centered around biblical principles and everyday life.

Traveling Teachers

A second innovative ministry that Grace Bible Fellowship started was what they called the "traveling teacher." Losing their Christian school building opened up an opportunity for a truly fresh approach to education. Instead of trying to continue with a Christian school, they sent the teachers into homes to equip the parents to teach their children. Each teacher visited households on a rotational basis to provide assistance, encouragement, and accountability. The parents thus began to grow in their confidence to teach their own children.

Primary Responsibility

Elder and teacher John Thompson sees his responsibility as primarily being one of building up the men in his church. Good relationships are important because within them men can accept the teaching without feeling threatened. Each day John tries to have several contacts with men, either by phone or face-to-face. Periodically, he leads a men's discipleship class. In the past, he has used these informal times to teach men on topics such as, how to study the Bible, debt, home business, how to prepare for worship, how to study theology, and prayer. As part of a typical Sunday morning worship service fathers are given time to share from the Word and lead in a hymn or prayer.

"Without a doubt, fathers embracing leadership in the home and in the church are the greatest benefits of household ministry." From this basic benefit come others. Because the men lovingly lead, women are free to use their gifts and abilities to serve. Children grow in their appreciation of the biblical role models seen in their parents. Young men in particular pattern their lives after their fathers. Some as young as fifteen stand up before the assembly and bring teaching or prayer.

Selecting People to Lead Programs

As part of a transition strategy the following guidelines for selecting people to lead programs may prove helpful.

First, try to select whole households where possible. This avoids segregation and gives household heads the opportunity to observe and determine others' gifts in a ministry relationship. Use of gifts, not guilt-induced coercion, are the best way to involve people in ministry.

If someone does not come forward to lead a program, then consider that it might be God's way of saying that a particular program is not needed at that time. Galatians 6:1-2 calls us to be responsive to needs in the church. It is surprising how often needs can be met without a program.

Some thought must be given to the home-life of the people who want to help. People are already overloaded with hectic schedules. Households need time together, which means they need freedom. They need to know that it is acceptable to lay aside ministry responsibilities in order to stay at home and work with their households. To avoid such overload, which can occur if this approach is dumped on top of an existing approach, churches should seek to start in small, calculable ways, such as introducing an age-integrated Sunday school class. Starting small allows people to ease into the transition and develop a core group of people who can help implement the approach more broadly in the future.

Developing Synergy Among Programs

A crucial way to improve current programs is to develop a synergy that ties all ministries together around a common goal or theme. This has the effect of focusing people toward God's perspective. This can be especially helpful to churches that hang on to age-segregated approaches. Even if members of the household are split up, there will be enough synergy between what is learned that they will be able to talk through it and make life applications through the week.

Benefits and Implications

The overall benefits of a household approach for church leaders and staff are more freedom, more personal involvement and maturity.

For pastors, elders, deacons (leaders)

Leaders will focus on discipling the men of the congregation (1 Timothy 3; Titus 2). Leaders' wives will focus on discipling the women (Titus 2). Leading couples can focus on other couples or individuals. This will involve the leaders assigning households for individual accountability, such as can be done through small groups. Early-morning breakfasts, lunches, or even dinner meetings can be helpful. A modest budget to help defray the costs of travel, food, etc. should be considered. This may seem ambitious. Remember Jesus discipled twelve men in only three years. As men are discipled, more of them will become elders, at least in function if not in official title.

For staff

Staff will be free to meet several rudimentary priorities that commonly get squeezed out by the current cacophony of activities. They will be able to spend copious amounts of time reading, meditating, and praying for the church members and how they might better serve them. They will be able to spend more time focusing on relationships so that heart-level ministry can happen and maturity can be realized.

Household leadership development becomes a high priority. More fruit can be achieved by focusing on one person, who can then take the same teaching and work much more effectively with one, two, three, or more people in the home!

By streamlining and reorienting activities to have a household focus, the staff can plan and work in unison with other ministries to accomplish stated common core goals in such a way that efforts are not doubled.

For parents

Parents will be free to spend time developing household relationships. In particular, they will have a much clearer picture of what "church" can offer. Ministry will be more targeted, with ability to measure results through personal accountability. Integrating programs will actually make it easier to focus on household leadership because the household will be working together. More mature leaders will be developed. The time that is freed up can be used by parents to work within their own households or other church members.

As we close this book, let us turn our attention now to some powerful testimonies of how this approach has helped people become spiritually strong and mature leaders.

Churches across the nation are discovering that this approach works. This chapter draws on the wisdom and testimony of church leaders who are boldly integrating the church and home — and building effective Christians.

A Household of Overcomers

c h a p t e r 15

"And they overcame him [Satan] because of the blood of the Lamb and because of the word of their testimony and they did not love their life even to death" (Revelation 12:11).

In Revelation, the apostle John tells us that our victory over Satan comes as a result of Christ and the testimony of the people living in His power. These are people whose lives are conduits of Christ's love, living not to please themselves but to serve others. Through Christ, we have the example and power to live as overcomers, but we must reach out and grab it. This means changing the way we minister so that we can capitalize on that power.

Not too long ago, ABC ran a special one-hour program about the McCaughey family from Cedar Point, Iowa. You may remember that this is the family that had septuplets in 1997. It did not take too long to learn that the McCaugheys were Christians, who saw each of their children as blessings, even though they faced miles of seemingly insurmountable challenges. As the story unfolded it was clear that their church was right there with them through this whole experience—and showed no signs of letting up. Their church organized twenty-four-hour shifts to care for the children so that Mom and Dad could get some sleep. They were there to help change diapers, feed, bathe, and rock the children to sleep. One man even came to help after working on his farm all day. These people were clearly sacrificing, out of love, to help the family.

The interviewer was incredulous as to how the McCaugheys would cope as time passed, but it became apparent that the church was there to help them as long they needed it, and in fact, the family would do just fine. It is precisely this example of sacrificial love that I think Paul had in mind when he wrote that "they will know we are Christians by our love." Is it not part of our calling from God to reveal His glory through our relationships?

Churches who walk the path of household-based ministry experience tremendous blessings. One such blessing is the integrated, involved community life. Blane Hamner, a single from Redeemer PCA church in Madison, Alabama, found that "The intergenerational approach makes me more a part of the church. I am able to get to know all the people in the church. And because I'm more of a part, I'm willing to do more. Before, it was easier not to get involved. Now, everyone takes care of everybody else."

How is Blane benefiting from household ministry? "I'm more consistent in my prayer life and scripture reading because it's more challenging to me. It has helped me address questions of leadership like how to treat my wife and children—before I get married. It has made me address issues that required forward thinking. I have never been challenged that way before."

Pastors are finding themselves meeting challenges head on that have been difficult to meet before—such as the challenge of finding able people to help. A focus on households raises household heads to lead their families. Pastor Stewart Jordan capitalizes on this. He doesn't have a staff in the traditional sense. In his monthly "Head of Household Meetings," he reminds the heads that they are "the staff," "that their meetings are governmental meetings," and that "they are the ministry team of the church." "By integrating their household management with the work of eldering, it helps maintain a connection between leadership in the church with day-to-day leadership in the home." This simplifies ministry planning but also places the emphasis where it should be—on household leaders. Elder John Thompson agrees with this approach, saying that "it is a blessing for fathers to articulate vision which includes the wife as primary helper and children as team members."

Many hurting families are looking for those that have it together. It makes sense, then, to use families in outreach. Pastor Roach's church began applying household principles about five years ago. Since that time they have been undergoing a far-reaching transformation. For instance, last Easter, instead of having their traditional four-night and two-Sunday-service Passion Play extravaganza, they modified it to a one-service "Family Celebration of the Resurrection." They involved every member of the church's households—even the three- to five-year-olds. Instead of seeing about forty people come to faith in Christ, this year saw 110!

In other ministries, Bob reports a new joy and expectation on the part of their households. "There is new vision that we are the household of God and unity based upon life that comes through our unique and rejuvenated cell group ministry." Rejuvenated because their basis is to use cell groups, not as glorified Bible studies, but to build relationships that love. By the way, their restructuring has now included program leaders becoming cell group leaders. When Calvary started this approach five years ago, there were only 250 people. Now they are up to a thousand. Bob attributes this growth to the principles of building heart-level relationships in households.

Ministry built upon relationships, not age-segregated programs, is growing as a better way to minister. "In order for any program to work, discipleship relationships must be built in. The classroom lecture-style approach fails because the present generation is biblically illiterate and has no biblical model in which to understand how what is taught can be applied to real life," says Harvester PCA pastor, Ron Bossom.

Building ministry around relationships frees people to take ownership of ministry. "People need to see their own fingerprints on ministry," says Elder John Thompson. There is a direct correlation between involvement and ownership. People "own" a vision when they help to form it and then play significant roles in implementing it. This stirs more of the right kind of involvement that we desire to see in ministry. People gathering together uninhibited by divisions provides a strong platform for unity to be developed in vision and in its outworking. "Ministry becomes more clearly focused. Instead of the fragmentation of a dozen different programs appealing to a dozen different needs, it becomes a single focus which blossoms into more time and freedom for ministry rather than endless meetings and planning."

People need freedom from performance-oriented living (and ministry). Carol, a churchgoing single, had a bitter relationship with her father growing up. "He had high expectations for me. When I conformed to his wishes, I was accepted, but when I didn't, I suffered rejection. I never seemed to get my father's approval, so I grew up angry and bitter. In my early twenties, I made a profession of faith at an Imperials concert and started receiving counseling at my local church. The approach of the church in counseling once again put me under a regimen of works acceptance and did not deal with the heart issue, which was that I hated my father.

"The struggles followed me into my job and my life turned worse. Then I was taken under wing by a pastor and his wife who began dealing with me not on behavioral issues but on the issue of the heart. By loving me, accepting me, and communicating God's acceptance of me because of the work of Christ, after only eight weeks, I realized that I needed to ask my father for forgiveness. I was free to confess my sin without condemnation. It is the acceptance that made it possible to come clean with my father. Shortly after this, my life began to change in a way that I'd never thought possible. My whole countenance was lifted and my job performance improved."

Pastor Ben Taylor says it well: "When involvement and outward conformity are what we stress in ministry, religion is externalized. Eventually, however, those things become less satisfying, and don't reach the soul. They have all the forms of godliness but without the power. A person who is busy doing lots of "great things for the Lord" can be mean-spirited, not yielding to the Holy Spirit, not concerned about the needs of others. They can become more concerned about getting ribbons from God. They equate obedience with blessing. But in John 1 we read that God rewards only on grace and this is much greater than working. We are therefore free to obey, not out of fear as under a harsh taskmaster, but out of delight in our salvation. We realize that the basis for our service is an outgrowth of our freedom in Christ and begin to rest in what is eternally true of them in Christ."

In the final analysis, when the dross is separated from the gold, what really matters is seeing hearts changed for the glory of Christ. Christ lived and died that our hearts may be redeemed from death and cleansed and opened to victorious, fulfilling life.

He would not have had to die if all we had to do was act right. The Pharisees tried that and failed.

By His life, death, and resurrection, Jesus showed us that the way to the heart is through relationships that are built upon love, enduring commitment, sacrifice, humility, and submission to the needs of others. This is a narrow path, but it is the right one. If we expect to see change in our hearts and in the hearts of those around us, we must model what we see in our Savior. We must have a deep desire to live for God in all ways and to help others do the same. We must obey the law of love.

This means evaluating all that we do, why we do it, and how we do it—not just in our own lives and households, but also in the church, God's household. Are we walking the path of our Savior in ministry? Are we seeking Him, or are we seeking our own desires?

We are at a point in history when we have an enormous opportunity to rebuild the household of God. If we take the opportunity, I believe that our children will see blessings beyond our wildest dreams. The testimonies of today will become the inheritances of tomorrow, and the truth that we are overcomers in Christ will prevail and shed light on generations to come.

Appendix

How To Appeal To Your Leaders

appendix A

This appendix is designed to offer some principles and guidelines to help individuals approach their leaders in a loving and honoring way. Please use this in conjunction with the material in chapter thirteen and fourteen.

If your intent is to approach your leaders on these issues, you and the members of your group should establish a relationship with the leadership team and let them know you would like to make an appeal. This eliminates the perception of subterfuge (Titus 2:7-8). Be up front with what you are doing from the start.

As a preliminary measure, consider giving your pastor articles, letters, or summarized outlines of what you will present. A personal-information campaign like this will help immeasurably in cultivating a mutual trust upon which you will need to work. If you do not already know your pastor well, then make it a point to get to know him better.

Leaders Are Shepherds; Followers Are Sheep

In the scriptures, church leaders are likened to shepherds. By contrast, you and I are likened to sheep. Sheep need the care of and accountability to their shepherds. To provide this care, God has endowed shepherds with an instinct of concern for influences that are, or appear to be, "new." Through our shepherds, God affords us the blessing of His protection from any "new" thing that is harmful.

Are These Concepts New to Your Pastor?

Like it or not, the issues discussed in this book are indeed new to many of our shepherds. Many pastors were not taught these issues in seminary, at least not to the degree we have discussed in this book. We must be wise as serpents but gentle as doves when presenting our concerns.

Some of you will experience a greater challenge because people before you did not present a biblical appeal. As a result, leaders and others in your church were left with a bitter taste in their mouth. You must seek to overcome this and win their support.

Presenting an Appeal

What should we do when we believe the direction of our leaders needs to be altered? For this God has graciously given us the appeal process, through which we can respectfully present our concerns. Notice, however, that the word here is "appeal." Ultimatums, loud voices, and red faces do not work very well.

Before actually appealing to your pastor, church staff member, elder board, or governing body, it is important to prepare yourselves. The following information is designed to help you do just that.

You Are Under Protective Authority

You must first understand your place under protective authority. "Obey your leaders and submit to them; for they keep watch over your souls, as those who will give an account. Let them do this with joy and not with grief, for this would be unprofitable"

(Hebrews 13:17).

Notice in this verse that we are commanded to obey and submit to our leaders. We all know that we are to obey those in civil authority. This command extends to the church leaders under whom you have voluntarily placed yourself. These leaders watch over and protect those under their authority. God holds them accountable for their exercise of this vital responsibility. It is in our best interests to follow the direction they give, unless their direction clearly contradicts God's commands.

When we choose not to follow our leaders, we stand outside of the protective authority God intended. The fiercely independent, prideful nature of most Americans today does not lend itself to being under authority. We must be careful not to give in to those sinful urges.

Check Your Attitude

You must be in right standing with your leaders before you make an appeal. An effective appeal is delivered out of the proper motives. Following are four key motivations that you must have.

1. Be concerned for the reputation of your leaders (Proverbs 22:1; Exodus 32:12).

After the sons of Israel sinned at Sinai, Moses appealed to God not to destroy the Israelites on the basis of His reputation. "Why should the Egyptians speak, saying, `With evil intent He brought them out to kill them in the mountains...' " Applying the principle to your situation, you may say something like this: "Pastor Mike, many people respect your commitment to households and think that applying these principles will help strengthen your standing as a pastor who is committed to households."

2. Be concerned for the goals of your leaders (Ephesians 4:12).

The primary goal of any pastor is to more effectively proclaim the gospel. One of Paul's goals was unity in Christ among the brethren. Pastors are very concerned about introducing elements into the ministry of the church that could spark division. Seek to show your pastor and leaders how what you are proposing will serve to develop greater unity among the people.

3. Appeal at the appropriate time (Esther 5:8).

Esther is a model of someone who chose the right time to appeal. Too often in our hurry-up, should-have-been-done-last-week world, we push through project after project. Sometimes after evaluation we discover that waiting may have been a better strategy. There are certainly better times than others to present an appeal. With this in mind choose the time you think would be best to present your appeal.

4. Be willing to sacrifice to help your leaders (Exodus 32:32).

Moses was willing to sacrifice himself in order to save the people from destruction. As part of the appeal process, plan to offer yourself to help your leaders. Be willing to do research for them or teach a Sunday school class. If you are not able to help, maybe you should find someone else to give the appeal.

Points to Include in Your Appeal

As we have seen, the attitude of the appeal is important! Basically, this whole book is an appeal. Use as much of it as you think will be helpful. Following are some key points you would do well to have clear answers for.

What shape will this ministry take? What specific activities will you propose to add (if any)? What programs or existing structures should be changed? In what order should they be changed? Think strategically.

Integration: How can a household approach strengthen the existing ministry? It is unhealthy to divide households into isolated cliques. It is therefore very important that you explain how this will help all members of the greater church household.

Scope of ministry: How will this ministry be a catalyst for outreach?

Follow-up

Once you have made your appeal, it is important to follow up. Continue to develop a relationship with your leaders. Establish a regular time to meet with them. Close communication is essential to avoid misunderstandings and build confidence and trust.

Avoid associations or postures that could be misunderstood. Do not do anything that would chip away the trust you have worked hard to establish.

If necessary, write up periodic reports for your leaders to inform them of progress.

Use wisdom in selecting special speakers. Do not try to sneak in a speaker whose views may be unacceptable to your leaders. Encourage a dialog between any outside speaker and the pastor at an early stage.

Handling Negative Responses

Should your appeal be turned down or met with a hostile response, do not despair. First, review the appeal process. Examine yourself for any inappropriate attitude, motivation, or sinful response to your leaders. Confess and seek your leaders' forgiveness if necessary.

Second, clearly document your leaders' concerns. Research these and report back to them with the information you have acquired. This keeps communication open.

Third, consider God's timing. Sometimes, for reasons that we do not understand, God's timing is different from our own. I remember working with a beleaguered mother in Indiana a few years back whose repeated attempts at starting a home-education ministry were met with frustration. After a lengthy conversation one evening, it became clear to me that God wanted this well-intentioned mother to spend her time working on relationships within her own household. God was therefore showing her mercy by not allowing her to get involved in a commitment that would have split her attention away from some important needs. Far too many people have lost their households in the process of doing great things to serve God. Do not be one of them.

The Home-Schooling Catalyst

a p p e n d i x B

What in the world does home-schooling have to do with household-based ministry? Without making household-based ministry sound like a "home-school" thing (because it is not—it is a biblical thing), I want to say, a lot. My purpose in this appendix is to show how home-schooling can be a catalyst for strengthening churches along the lines of household-based ministry. These concepts have proven helpful to many in bringing about reconciliation and unity in ministry development.

First, A Few Facts

In 1987 you could have stopped someone on the street and asked them what home-schooling was, and they might have looked at you strangely and said, "Home...what?" Today, just eleven years later, almost everybody knows someone who has chosen to home-school their children. Magazines and newspapers run feature articles interviewing home-schooling parents and their children.

A 1997 study entitled, *Strengths of Their Own*, conducted by

Dr. Brian Ray of the National Home Education Research Institute, shows that there are approximately 1.15 million children being home-schooled in the United States (Ray, p. 1). This figure is rising at about 15 percent per year (Ray, p. 2).

In its *Executive Summary of Home Education Across the United States*, the Home School Legal Defense Association reports that there are more home-school students nationally than there are total students in New Jersey, the state with the tenth largest public-school enrollment. There are also more home-school students nationwide than public-school students in Arkansas, Delaware, Hawaii, Montana, North Dakota, South Dakota, Rhode Island, Vermont, and Wyoming combined (Summary, p.2). Once largely a Christian movement, home-schooling is now practiced by people from all sectors of the American landscape (Summary, p.3).

Home-Schoolers Score Higher on Standardized Tests

The same Home School Legal Defense Association study reveals that home-school children score remarkably well on standardized tests. The average standardized test scores for home-schoolers is in the 87th percentile (Summary, p.2). The cost to home-school one student is an average $546 per year (Summary, p. 1). Ironically that is a savings of $4779 from the cost per public-school student ($5325), and home-school children score 37 percentile points better on standardized tests! (Summary pp. 1, 6).

Home-schooling Is Legal in All Fifty States

Each state has at least one major home-school organization that works to protect home-school freedoms legislatively and provide a range of services to its members. Newsletters, magazines, conventions, how-to-get-started workshops, and curriculum fairs are just a few examples.

What About Socialization?

Home-school children are far from being social couch potatoes. Many children finish their studies early in the day, making it possible to participate in a broad spectrum of outside activities, such as Scouts, ballet classes, 4-H clubs, volunteer work, ministry, Bible clubs, music classes, group sports, Sunday school, field trips, and many more (Ray, p. 50). In my work with home-schoolers over the past ten years, I can say that I am beyond impressed with the ability of these youngsters to communicate meaningfully with adults and others who are not in their immediate age group. This is an aspect of "socialization" that many people forget but is one of the most important if a child is going to function in society.

How Long Do They Home-School?

Most children (89%) home-school through twelfth grade (Summary, p.6). Of home-school graduates, 31% go directly into the workforce, while 69% go into post-secondary education, compared to public-school graduates at 29% and 71% respectively (Summary, p. 4). Most colleges accept home-school students. Home School Legal Defense Association maintains a running list of these institutions. The latest list I saw showed that home-schoolers have been accepted into 372 colleges, including major institutions such as Notre Dame, the University of Florida, Stanford, Harvard, and Yale.

Why Is Home-Schooling Successful?

Books have been written probing and examining the evidence. Empirically, there is no way to argue against the academic and social success of home-schooling. Home-schoolers compare quite favorably to public- and private-school children. What is it that makes home-schooling so successful? It is not money. We have already concluded that. It is not because parents are professionally certified teachers. The vast majority of home-schooling parents do not hold teaching certificates. It is due to parents who are making big sacrifices to give what they think is the best possible education to their children. Their heart-to-heart involvement and hard work is what makes home-schooling so successful.

Is There More to Home-Schooling Than Meets the Eye?

There is more to the home-schooling movement than mere academic achievement. In many home-school households you will find an understanding and appreciation for the concepts I have addressed in this book. Therefore, home-schooling and the local church should fit together like a hand in glove. I will address the how and why of this in a moment. Tragically, however, schisms have developed between some of these households and the typical church. Having been in the home-school movement myself for ten years, and in the ministry for equally as many, I have learned that the two are made up of very strong "D" personalities. Home-schoolers are dogmatic about how great home-schooling is, and pastors are dogmatic about their theology, doctrine, and church traditions.

Over the past six years, I have worked with hundreds of individuals and churches in an effort to mend these fences. Mending is one of the purposes of this book. Home-schoolers and pastors can play a pretty good game of tattletale. I have heard about some home-school households who have done a poor job of approaching their church leaders on the issue of home-schooling and household-based ministry. On the other hand, I have heard of pastors who have done an equally poor job responding to the inquiries of these households. This need not be. Prejudice, name-calling, and division is the work of the Evil One and should be denounced.

Thankfully, such antagonistic relationships are few. As a matter of fact, in his doctrinal dissertation entitled T*he Home School Movement and the Traditional Church*, Pastor Daniel Bartel states that of the pastors within his denomination, the Presbyterian Church in America (PCA), "...the overwhelming majority [who responded to his survey] indicated that they had experienced little or no conflict [with home-schooling]" (p. 135). Bartel attributes this remarkable statistic to the "PCA's theological paradigm, which emphasizes, by its nature, a covenantal relationship between parents and children" (Bartel, p. 135).

Based on his studies, Bartel suggests that the way to maintain a peaceful relationship between home-schooling and the church is to promote Christ-centered liberty and emphasize the covenantal responsibilities of parents to train their children. (Bartel, p. 136). Bartel's counsel flows right in line with the thrust of this book. A vision that emphasizes discipleship training beginning in the home is a vision that helps everybody (whether you home-school or not).

Four Influences

Home-schooling introduces the following influences into the local church, which in turn help produce revival in the household unit.

1. Parents are learners too.

Parents develop an understanding of themselves as learners and teachers who are accountable. To some, this assertion may sound ridiculously simple and insignificant. However, when you stop to think about it, schools and churches do fulfill a large part of the educational responsibility for children, leaving little for parents to do. The home-schooling stimulus gives parents a deeper understanding of their need to be equipped to teach their own children.

2. Academics are a tool for revealing heart issues.

Academic study is a tool for sanctification, through which parents are forced to deal with sins in themselves and their children. Academic pressures reveal the heart of the child and the parent! The disciplines of academic study put pressure on a child that exposes the true condition of his heart. Such discipline provides a window to the child's heart where character flaws can be seen in their most subtle forms. The teacher, whoever that happens to be, has the opportunity to deal with the character flaws that surface.

When Harvester Teaching Services began working with home-schoolers ten years ago, one mother made the following comment to me: "I had no idea the extensive nature of the battle that Satan was waging over the hearts of my children, until I brought them home." She was sitting at the window of their hearts and did not like what she saw! And these were children you would characterize as having it all together.

Most parents who home-school discover that the problems they must deal with are not merely those of their children. The hardest aspect of dealing with the sin in children is that it often reflects the same sin in the parents. In this sense, academic study is a mirror to the parent's heart. Many parents have recoiled at the thought of spending more time with their children because they know they will have to face their own sin. However, choosing to ignore what God reveals about our sin will inhibit the passing on of God's richest blessings to future generations.

3. Home-schooling provides a framework for developing relationships.

Many home-school households learn the importance of sticking together. In particular, many children learn to serve their brothers and sisters. This builds a framework for strong relationships within the household.

4. Everyday life-learning teaches Christianity as a lifestyle.

Opportunities to learn biblical truth as it relates to academics, relationships, and everyday life make it possible to experience Christianity as a consistent lifestyle. When these opportunities are shared in the context of the household unit, a vital foundation is laid upon which a strong multi-generational ministry can be built.

Opportunities to Apply Faith

As home-school students learn Christianity as a lifestyle, they develop a testimony that can be passed down through generations. They are learning to live, not learning simply to amass knowledge. Because their home and everyday activities become the backdrop or context for their education, they are keeping a practical handle on what is taught and are thereby living out the principles of Deuteronomy 6.

Academic study opens up opportunities to learn about the deeper truths of God's character. When the study of math, English, science, and history are grounded principally in God's Word, they become the tools that God intended people to have in order to rule the earth wisely.

For example, math is a study of following orderly processes. When we violate the order of steps in solving a math problem, we get a wrong answer. Through such study we learn that God is a God of order. Everything we do should be done in an orderly fashion if God is to be glorified.

To illustrate further, God is the author of history. Every event takes place at His approval. The sovereignty of God is a primary principle that we can learn through studying how God has used specific events in history to establish His plan.

A good resource to help parents understand these principles comes from Paul Jehle, of the New Covenant Christian School in Buzzards Bay, Massachusetts. He has done some extraordinary work for parents in his newsletter, *Renewing the Mind*. In each issue, he takes a particular academic discipline and expounds upon the biblical principles that can be taught through it.

Five Strengths Gained from Home-Schooling Households

The influence of home-schooling households helps the church strengthen its ministry in five ways:

1. By focusing on equipping parents to teach their children instead of doing it for them.
2. By teaching theology and doctrine in the context of practical everyday life.
3. By rediscovering the sufficiency of the discipleship process for bringing Christians to maturity.
4. By providing a practical perspective on a number of topics relating to the household, relationships, academics, and so on.
5. By setting before the church a powerful example of strong and healthy relationships through households.

For some the path to a household ministry approach begins with what I call a home-education ministry. It should be remembered that even in a home-education ministry, home-schooling should not be the core issue. The core issue is equipping parents and others to disciple their children and others for maturity and leadership of future generations.

Challenges

a p p e n d i x C

Many questions and concerns will no doubt surface as the material in this book is considered in its entirety. My goal, however, in this section is to deal with some common concerns that often surface when applying the principles in this book to current programs and systems. We need to see making changes as a way of being more obedient to God. This is the only thing that will help us stick with our plan during the difficult times.

Nine Challenges

Challenge #1: Fear of change.

Fear is often ignorance in disguise. The material in this book should help in understanding household ministry. But fear of change is no reason not to change. Fear of this sort is also a sin (Isaiah 41:10) that has as its root distrusting that God will do what He promises.

A well-conceived plan that is communicated with conviction will greatly reduce this potential trap. It is important to remember that this will not be an all-or-nothing proposition, nor will it happen overnight; it will take as much time as God wants it to.

Challenge #2: Changing ministry habits.

Like all change, it will be challenging to do things differently at first. When tests come, you must stick with the plan and not fall back into old ministry habits. This is why it is necessary to begin with a clear picture of what you are trying to achieve. This includes both a clear vision and a clear plan for how you are going to achieve it. A clear vision and plan are two key components to winning the involvement of others within the church. If everybody, especially the leaders, are in agreement, then there is a built-in accountability and encouragement not to give up and fall back into old habits.

Challenge #3: Communicating this new approach.

Communicating this approach needs to be done in love and with great care. It must be done thoroughly with consistent follow-up and refinement. You must resolve to follow through and not let the primacy of communicating this vision be undermined by the tyranny of the urgent. If we fail at this level, then we will be fighting an uphill battle.

Challenge #4: Meeting the time element for church leaders.

Church leaders will need time to expand their discipleship ministry in order to meet with individual household leaders regularly (breakfast, lunch, or dinner) to develop a deep relationship with them, encourage them, and hold them accountable. If each elder, for instance, focuses on just one father at a time, the potential for developing future church leaders doubles! This does not include the children of those fathers who will indirectly benefit. Those fathers who become elders themselves will be challenged to work with other fathers to disciple them. Over time, as more elders and church leaders are trained, the burden on the present leadership will be diminished.

Challenge #5: Nurturing a burden in the hearts of parents and other household leaders to reach out to other members of God's household.

To overcome this challenge you must emphasize relationships. We all need to understand that our responsibility extends beyond our own households to widows, orphans, singles, single-parent households, and others who need to be part of a household (Psalm 68:6). If the church cannot effectively integrate these individuals, then the church will be functionally irrelevant to answering the problems of our day.

You must grapple with the reasons why fathers especially do not take this step. The number-one factor is that fathers lack vision due to inadequate training. Unfortunately, very little in our lives happens because we are motivated by a vision; most of what happens is an emotional response to our circumstances.

To the contrary, what should be happening is making wisdom-based decisions that are an outgrowth of a continually developed vision.

Overcoming stress. Occupied by the stresses of the everyday rat-race life (which includes a fair amount of self-gratification), we all struggle to develop a vision for our lives, much less find the time to minister to others on a personal level. Loving one another (John 13:34) is not a one-way activity. Each person gives and each person receives (Acts 2:45). Ministering to an individual in a household requires that person to minister back and actually gives him the greatest freedom to reciprocate.

Overcoming Busyness. Not all busyness is necessary; nor is it productive. Busyness thrives where there are no clear priorities. Many people are too busy doing things that are good but are not the most important. They need to be challenged in light of their biblical priorities to change their busyness.

Overcoming fear. Weak leaders do not want people to see what really happens behind closed doors. While opening the doors may be embarrassing, leaving them closed and ignoring the problems inside will not make them go away. This situation is indeed tragic when you consider the generational implications.

Another occasion for fear is that many feel inadequate to lead their own households spiritually, let alone those who might be added to the household.

Being free. Parents and household leaders are often not free to pursue these relationships. The first step in gaining this freedom is to develop a vision and commitment for household relationships. This is a matter of obedience within the church community. This in effect raises a standard for them to work toward.

The second step is to help people streamline their schedule. This should be a priority anyway, and it will become easier as the church tries to keep the household together in ministry. A streamlined schedule means more freedom to pursue relationship opportunities.

The third step is to help parents see that extraordinary plans and considerations are not necessarily required. A simple plan to include another person in an already planned activity is a solid start.

In the case of singles this can be easily done. Some households may already have singles living with them. Seeking to envelop them into household life is therefore easier.

Integrated programs can be a real help in developing relationships by providing "ice-breakers" and opportunities for structure.

Challenge #6: Building a burden for our neighborhoods.

Because ministry has been associated for such a long time with the church building, many Christians have lost a vision for their neighborhoods. In Acts 1:8 the disciples were reminded of their role as witnesses in Jerusalem, and in all Judea and Samaria, and even to the remotest parts of the earth. Their first place of concern was to be Jerusalem. We should be most concerned about the people God regularly puts in our path. It is also much more efficient to work within our neighborhoods.

The approach to neighbors must emphasize relationships. This is not a panacea. It takes focused effort. It is in some ways more difficult than having a Bible study or vacation Bible school. Not that those are wrong. It is clear, however, that the average American is looking for deeper relationships, which are often difficult to express through programs alone.

Praying about and choosing just one neighbor with which to develop a relationship can make such a difference. Inviting them over for meals, going out for activities, maybe even including them on vacations is a great way to spend time with them and develop a bond of trust wherein deeper issues can be shared and the healing balm of the gospel can be applied. This does not occur quickly! Indeed it can take a long time. Imagine the effect that winning a whole household to God would mean over generations!

Challenge #7: Some children do not want to be with their parents. Putting them together will cause problems.

It is not wrong for children to want to be with other people. Under certain conditions, it is OK for children to be with other children. Clearly, however, this desire is not always pure and should not be accommodated in such cases. When the constant cry is to be away from the parents, one should expect that there is a problem in the relationship. Our culture idolizes individualism and is hypersensitive to the youth subculture. Rebellion toward parents is a common theme. We cannot discount the destructive impact of these combined factors in our Christian homes!

Rebellion is NOT normal. It is typical, however. We must begin to reject the behavioral psychologists who sold our culture on the theory that teenage rebellion is normal and to be expected. There are no biblical grounds for this claim, but age-segregation tends to accommodate this sinful understanding. In order to remedy this, consider: the seeds of rebellion are sown over time, beginning when children are very young. To continue to respond to the results of rebellion is to perpetuate the problem for yet more generations.

Therefore the church should help parents develop a vision and lifestyle that puts a priority on developing heart-level relationships with all of their children. This will help preclude the problems which often come up later in the teen years. This relationship should continue with even greater fervor in the teen years. When the relationship is strong, and love is an indicator, the framework is there for the child to accept the scriptural basis as something that is good for him. When relationships are poor, the scripture is often rejected. Perhaps a reason for this is that the father is doing a poor job representing God the Father before his children.

Once the seeds of rebellion grow roots, it is hard to pluck them up. Doing so requires a sacrificial love and perseverance. Over time, as parents strengthen their relationships with their children, the concerns aroused by children who do not want to be with their parents will evolve into cries to be with them.

Challenge #8. A household approach which focuses on one-on-one discipleship relationships violates 2 Corinthians 9:6: "Now this I say, he who sows sparingly shall also reap sparingly and he who sows bountifully shall also reap bountifully."

This verse is often used as a basis for the church to do more in order to bring more people into the church. I believe that we should do what we can to introduce people to Christ and disciple them to maturity. But what does this belief mean in light of this principle of sowing and reaping?

As His servants, we all rejoice at seeing another lost sinner come to faith in Christ. We revel in the fruit of their resulting sanctification. God rejoices and commands us to be His tools in this life-changing process. Are we doing enough? Let us consider this scripture in light of this question.

This specific verse does not appear elsewhere in scripture, although the sentiment does. The context of this verse has Paul appealing to the Corinthian church to give money with liberality. The verse in question is an attempt to help them see that giving liberally, not out of compulsion, will cause them to reap liberally. (Although it is not a command to increase activities in an effort to increase the size of the church membership, let us consider the principle.)

Principle or absolute?

If we sow bountifully does that guarantee a bountiful harvest? Is this a principle or an absolute? Analogy: If a man invests all of his $10,000 savings in the stock market (sowing bountifully) in order to get a big return, is he guaranteed to get it (reap bountifully)? He may actually reap bountifully, doubling his money in two years, but he is not guaranteed even the slightest return. It is also possible that he may invest only $1000 (sow sparingly) and in one year gain $4000 (reap bountifully!) Analogy: If a student spends ten hours studying his math in preparation for an exam (sowing bountifully) is he assured of getting an A? He may. He may not. Analogy: Proverbs 22:6 says that if we train up a child in the way he should go he will not depart from it. Is this an absolute statement? Many parents do their best to train their children, only to find their children stray for a period of time or make a colossal mistake that changes the course of their life.

What does it mean to sow and reap bountifully? Does it only mean having a lot of activities that will bring a lot of people into the church? In this case, sowing and reaping is a quantitative pursuit and appears to have no basis (as a motivation for ministry) in scripture. Or does sowing and reaping mean investing great amounts of time in building godly character into people so that they are more mature? In this case, sowing and reaping is a qualitative pursuit and has great support in scripture (James 1:22; 1 Timothy 1:5; Philippians 4:8-9; 2 Peter 1:3-9) and sometimes results in great numbers.

We often cling to certain programs because they appear on the organizational chart as outreaches into the community or are means of sowing bountifully. We often look at these programs as non-negotiable, as if the principle of sowing and reaping were an absolute, when in fact, the ability of the programs themselves to bring people in may be in question.

Consider that you may actually be sowing bountifully and reaping bountifully and not know it because you are clinging to an unbiblical idea about what these mean.

Integrated programs that are in balance with household relationships help the church reach out to our communities while building maturity in its members. How might we change existing programs to increase the possibility of qualitative growth?

Challenge #9. How does this approach help people at different levels of maturity?

The household approach enables the church to actually do a better job of ministering to people at different levels of maturity because it places a high value on personal discipling relationships. Relationships provide a personal framework within which an individual's spiritual condition can be known, challenged, and developed. We could never design enough programs to deal with everyone's specific situation. Programs, however, can provide a valuable contribution to this discipleship process.

Bibliography

Bork, Robert H. *Slouching Towards Gomorrah: Modern Liberalism and American Decline.* New York, NY: Harper Collins, 1996.

McDowell, Josh. *Right From Wrong: What You Need to Know to Help Youth Make Right Choices.* Dallas, TX: Word, 1994.

Ptacek, Kerry. *Family Worship: Biblical Basis, Historical Reality, Current Need*. Greenville, SC: Presbyterian Theological Seminary, 1994.

Ray, Brian. *Strenghts of Their Own:* Home Schoolers Across America: Academic Achievement, Family Characteristics, & Longitutdianl Traits. Salem, OR: NHERI Publications, 1997.

Richards, Lawrence O. Christian Education: *Seeking to Become Like Jesus Christ*. Grand Rapids, MI: Zondervan, 1975.

Schlect, Christopher. Critique of Modern Youth Ministry. Moscow, ID: Cannon Press, 1995.

Schultz, Thom and Joani. *Why Nobody Learns Anything at Church Anymore: And How to Fix It.* Loveland, CO: Group Publishing, 1994.

Snyder, Howard A. *Liberating the Church*. Downers Grove, Ill: InterVarsity Press, 1983.

Order Information

To order more copies of *Uniting Church and Home,* or to inquire about quantity discounts or expedited delivery, please contact Solutions at the number below.

Solutions for Integrating Church and Home
P.O. Box 630
Lorton, Virginia 22199
Phone: 571-642-0071 Fax: 571-642-0079
Email: Solution77@sprynet.com